ROCHESTER, October 1847.

Rev. MR. CHEESEMAN:

Dear Sir—Having listened to your several lectures on the differences between what is termed "OLD AND NEW DIVINITY," with no little degree of interest, and believing that their publication at this time, will do great good to the cause of truth in Western New-York,—we would therefore, very respectfully, ask of you the same for publication.

While we remain,

Truly and Respectfully, Yours.

GABRIEL LONGMUIR,	DONALD CAMPBELL,
ALEX. LONGMUIR,	IRA COOK,
ROBERT PENNEY,	ROBERT FINLEY,
ANGUS McDONALD,	DAVID HUTCHINSON,
JAMES HUTCHINSON,	E. DARROW,
T. B. FORSYTH,	M. BALDWIN.

GENTLEMEN:

At your request, I send you the discourses on the differences between Old and New School Presbyterians, and as they were at first prepared for the pulpit and not for the press; I have concluded to omit the formalities with which they were delivered, and to present them in an abridged form, lest they should occupy too much space to be patiently read.

With an earnest desire that they may provoke examination and promote the peace, unity and purity of the Church,

I remain Gentlemen, Respectfully,

Yours in the best bonds,

LEWIS CHEESEMAN.

DIFFERENCES

BETWEEN

OLD AND NEW SCHOOL

PRESBYTERIANS

BY REV. LEWIS CHEESEMAN,
Pastor of the First Presbyterian Church, in connection with the
General Assembly, Rochester, N. Y.

WITH AN INTRODUCTORY CHAPTER,

BY JOHN C. LORD, D. D.
Pastor of the First Presbyterian Church, Buffalo, N. Y.

"That they all may be one; as thou Father art in me, and I in thee, that they also may be one in us: that the world may believe that thou hast sent me."—John xvii. 21.

PUBLISHERS
Eugene, Oregon

Wipf and Stock Publishers
199 W 8th Ave, Suite 3
Eugene, OR 97401

Differences between Old and New School Presbyterians
By Cheeseman, Lewis
ISBN: 1-59752-252-X
Publication date 6/10/2005
Previously published by Erastus Darrow, 1848

CONTENTS.

INTRODUCTION.

CHAPTER I.

THE ECCLESIASTICAL DIFFERENCES BETWEEN OLD AND NEW SCHOOL PRESBYTERIANS.

The secession—Its causes—Changes in Church government and operations by the New School no improvement—Separation necessary to a reformation.

CHAPTER II.

DOCTRINAL DIFFERENCES BETWEEN OLD AND NEW SCHOOL PRESBYTERIANS.

Sufferings of Christ—The New School deny their penal nature—They were penal.

CHAPTER III.

DOCTRINAL DIFFERENCES CONTINUED.

Imputation—What intended by it—Denied by the New School—The doctrine defended—New School views of faith exposed and refuted.

CHAPTER IV.

DOCTRINAL DIFFERENCES CONTINUED.

The Atonement—Its sufficiency—The New School limit it in its nature—The differences respect its nature, not its extent.

CHAPTER V.

DOCTRINAL DIFFERENCES CONTINUED.

Natural depravity—Denied by the New School—Its importance—Its denial dangerous.

CHAPTER VI.

DOCTRINAL DIFFERENCES CONTINUED.

The despensation of the Spirit—The New School by their views of ability and depravity, make the Spirits despensation void—They make truth an agent.—The Spirit the only agent in regeneration—They place infants on a level with mere annimals.

CHAPTER VII.

DOCTRINAL DIFFERENCES CONTINUED.

Revivals of Religion—Views of the Old School on this subject—Differences respecting their nature and genuineness.

CHAPTER VIII.

DOCTRINAL DIFFERENCES CONTINUED.

Tendencies of the new divinity—The new divinity rests upon one or at most two assumptions, both of which are false—Tends to infidelity.

CHAPTER IX.

BASIS OF UNION AMONG PRESBYTERIANS.

What it is—The New School have departed from it—A return necessary to a union.

CHAPTER X.

PLEA FOR UNION AMONG PRESBYTERIANS.

A union desirable—Division among Christians an evil—The true remedy proposed.

INTRODUCTION.

In the following work, the Rev. Mr. CHEESEMAN has designed to give a brief account of those doctrinal differences which separate Presbyterians of the Old and New School. Not that these differences are peculiar to Presbyterians, for the same contest between truth and error, is developed in some form in all those protestant denominations in which vitality enough remains, to resist the progress of error and spiritual decay; not that the questions between the adherents of the old and new divinity, are of modern origin; novelties now for the first time considered and debated, but because the ancient heresies which have been privily brought in and which have corrupted so large a portion of the Presbyterian communion, are still artfully concealed under various disguises from the eyes of multitudes of pious persons who could they be made to see them in their true deformity, would not tarry a night under their shadow. The adherents of the new Theology, sometimes represent, that there is really no substantial difference between their system and old divinity; that it is a meres logomachy, a difference in mode of expression and in philosophical explanations; again, with a strange yet characteristic inconsistency, they caricature the doctrines of grace and of the confession of faith as though they embodied all that was inconsistent, perverse and monstrous. Could it be made to appear to that large and respectable body of members of the Presbyterian Church, who though sound in the faith, yet remain in the New School connexion, that the principles for which the General Assembly contend and in the defence of which, they intended to bear their testimony in the excision act of 1837, are the same maintained by Paul the Apostle against the gainsayers of his day, the same afterward defended in the fifth century by Augustine, against Pelagius, and the same which were revived by Luther, and with which, as with a battle axe, he smote the gates of the great apostacy, they would not and could not give support and countenance, aid and comfort to the enemies of the truth by remaining an hour within the ecclesiastical walls of the the New School General Assembly. Yet if there be any thing clear which may be determined beyond all doubt, it is that the theological contest between the Reformers and the Romanists in the sixteenth century, is the same now waged between Old and New School Presbyterians. No intelligent reader can peruse the controversy between Luther and Dr. Eck, the champion of the Papists, without perceiving this. No degree of prejudice or blindness can conceal the fact, it is written as with a sunbeam, it is graven as with the point of a diamond in the face of a rock.

The *ability* for which Eck and the Romanists contended against the Reformers is precisely both in *form and substance* the same as that insisted upon by the new school divines.— The doctrines maintained by all the reformed churches have been rejected by them for the theological tenets of the Papacy. Nothing can be demonstrated by history if D'Aubigne's account of the Reformation does not establish this. Here was the cause of the division in the Presbyterian church.

The act of the General Assembly, whatever may be said of its regularity or expediency, as to form, time and place was prompted by a love of the truth, and was believed to be necessary to a suitable defence of the faith once delivered to the saints. The Presbyterian Church has ever manifested a Catholic Spirit, she claims no divine right to leave other churches to the uncovenanted mercies of God, which are no mercies at all. She admits the validity of the ordinations and ordinances of all evangelical churches who defend the doctrines of grace, even when that defence is confined to a remnant after the election of grace. She stands and has ever stood, both in Scotland and in the United States, for the truth, and wherever she finds it she loves and fellowships all who receive and maintain it. She acknowledges that the church Catholic and Universal is composed of all true believers by whatever name called or in whatever ecclesiastical connexion found. It was upon doctrinal questions deemed fundamental, that the Presbyterian Church consented to the dismemberment of nearly one half her entire connexion.— On the one hand were numbers, wealth and power, on the other the truth. For Christ's cross and crown she hesitated not to make the sacrifice. The Presbyterian Church might have struggled along, as have other denominations, holding together by her government, without any real agreement in doctrine and order, and it is sufficiently evident that the division in this great communion, was the result of the maintainance on the one hand and the rejection on the other, of the doctrines of the Reformers and of the Reformed churches. It would be easy to show how the same defence of the faith is perpetuating in other churches a conflict, the bitterness of which has been greatly mitigated among Presbyterians by their division into two bodies. Those who differ on radical points, can love each other better across a denominational division than when bound in the same yoke; for the "contentions of brethren are like the bars of a castle," and "how can two walk together except they be agreed."

The great questions at the Reformation were human depravity and ability. Says, the eloquent Historian, of the Reformation, "The inability of man and the Almighty power of God were the two truths Luther sought to reestablish."

"A man," says Luther in one of his first propositions against the Romish Theology, "who is a stranger to the grace of God, cannot keep the commandments of God. The will of man without divine grace is not free but enslaved and willing to be so."

" The Papists with Pelagius," says D'Aubigne, " asserting man's freedom would keep him in slavery, the Reformers showing him his fetters and how they may be struck off, were the true advocates of liberty, the questions were BETWEEN A LIBERTY PROCEEDING FROM MAN'S NATURE and a liberty that cometh from God." Such was the contest says this historian, in St. Paul's time, in the days of Augustine, and again in those of Luther; and such we may add is the controversy now between the old and new theology. Denying the representative character of Adam and the condemnation of mankind in him ; rejecting the doctrine of the innate universal moral alienation of our race from God ; giving to fallen man the power of obedience to the broken law, of self recovery, and of self regeneration; the adherants of the new divinity are upon the ground of the Romanists, of Eck their champion, and of Pelagius. The foundation of the atonement is subverted, the work of the Holy Spirit is despised, and man is *brought to himself* and to his own efforts and works for salvation rather than to God and to Christ.

The doctrines received by the reformers and contained in sacred Scriptures may be resolved into five points.

1. Apostacy, original sin, and human ability.
2. Grace in conversion or regeneration the sole work of God.
3. Justification by faith through Jesus Christ, who was made sin for us whose righteousness is imputed to the believer and received by faith alone.
4. The eternal election, and,
5. Perseverance of the saints.

All these truths stand related to and are dependant upon the first proposition ; hence the controversy between the Reformers and the Papists, was first upon this point, "*Whether man possessed in his own nature the power of loving God and doing righteousness."* The very first proposition of Luther, which made the ears of men to tingle ; the first blow struck upon the walls of Rome, whose reverberations resounded through Europe, was a denial of this docrine. Who stands with Luther now ? Surely not the New School Presbyterians, who in general, are abhorent of the sentiments of Luther and take ground with the Romanists, with a violence and denunciation almost equal to theirs. They hold up to scorn and contempt this very proposition of man's inability to any spiritual good in the mouths of their Old School brethren, and seem to think the whole gospel is in the dogma of human ability, as though the atonement was a free, full and sufficient sacrifice, NOT IN ITS OWN NATURE, but in the nature and ability of man himself.

As in Germany, France, Switzerland, and England the formulas of the Reformation are still professed by churches which are either Arminean or Socinion, and have long been known to be such ; so the Westminister confession is still retained by those who reject its distinctive features and doctrines. There are two reasons for this : the one is, error does not appear well in the consecutive order of a confession of faith ; it does not bear the exposure and so shrinks from the light. The other is found in the advantages gained by assaulting truth under the shelter of an orthodox creed. At the beginning "they privily brought in damnable heresies." No stab is so sure, so effectual, as that which is given in the disguise of a friend ; no open war is so dangerous or so deadly as household treason. Enough has been heard of human ability in the popular preaching of the present day rung on innumerable changes ; enough has been seen of the ridicule attempted to be cast on the doctrine of original sin and native depravity ; enough of that hortatory and empty sermonizing which instead of exhibiting the great doctrines of the gospel, is ever declaiming upon human ability and human powers ; enough of that kind of faith which is made to terminate in what the creature can do, rather than what God can do and has done; enough of this wood, hay and stubble which is destined to the fire, has been manifest to render it an unnecessary labor to extract from the sermons, discussions and controversies of the day, further proof of this departure from the faith. But that all may see that we are dealing with realities and speaking of things not of a former age or among another generation, the following account of the recent examination of a candidate in Thelogy, is extracted from the Presbyterian.

"It has happened to me lately to attend an ordaining council in Massachusetts, and as the views of theology, developed by the examination of the candidate, are generally understood to be the same as now taught at Andover, indeed one of the Professors of that Institution was a member of the council, and as it was publicly declared, that this young man was as sound as half the ministers of the State, it is certainly proper that the Christian public should know what these views are.

1. There was a full denial of original sin. Sin was defined to be actual transgression exclusively. The term original sin might be used, but altogether in an another sense ; signifying only such a disordered state, that the first moral act would be sinful. But this *bias* is not transgression, is not sin, and does not expose to eternal punishment. And indeed, whatever original sin is, God is its author. No such thing as *desert* can be predicated of a creature before moral action.

2. He asserted, that nothing in original sin infringed a man's liberty to do good as well as evil. Every man has the same full and perfect ability to obey the whole law of God, that the questioner had to walk to the door. It is only to form the same determination of the will in the one case, as in the other. " There is no foundation of evil back of the will."

3. He denied the vicarious atonement. Christ did in no sense obey the law for us : nor did He suffer the penalty for our sins. The law of God will stand for ever a broken law, having never received the obedience which it demands, nor

the penalty which it denounces upon the transgressor. The work of Christ had no respect to this, but was a something else substituted for it. And men are justified, not by the righteousness of Christ imputed to them, but "in consequence of the sufferings of Christ :" the phrase of Dr. Dewey and the Unitarians.

4. He denied any direct and immediate influence of the Holy Spirit on the heart in regeneration. Regeneration is through the truth, and cannot be without the truth, and a mind capable of understanding it. Faith and repentance are produced by a knowledge of the truth, and *are themselves regeneration.* There is no direct act of the Holy Spirit upon the heart apart from the presentation of the truth : i. e. "moral suasion."

However, he would not say, that an infant could not be changed before becoming a sinner ; i. e. before actual transgression. God can create a new spirit ; and so he supposed it not beyond His *power* to change one already created.— But he did not know how such a change could be effected, nor did he think such a change probable. If so changed, it would not be holy, but only have the tendency to holiness. The first act of such an infant would be holy : *it would never become a sinner, and would never need a Saviour from sin :* nor could it be saved from actual sin.

He said also that as regeneration consisted in the change of faith and repentance, there might be fifty different modes of effecting it.

I submit this bold denial of the faith without note or comment, only saying that such views as these are alarmingly prevalent in New England, and on some points are known with certainty to be entertained by the new Professor of Theology at Andover."

The Romish doctors who resisted Luther, never departed so far from the truth. The theology of the Council of Trent, is hardly so corrupt or so barefaced a denial of the doctrines of the gospel. Yet with some reservations, evasions and apologies, the New York Evangelist, the organ of the New School Presbyterians, substantially vindicates this denial of "the faith once delivered to the saints," and caricatures after the manner of the Romish divines the very doctrines which are plainly taught in the confession of faith, which every Presbyterian minister subscribes at his ordination!

If we are not able to bring the questions before the Christian public in the usual controversial way, we can yet appeal to the piety of all who love our Lord Jesus, and receive him as the "the author and finisher of their faith," the "end of the law for righteousness to every one that believeth." It is one of the arts of errorists, to cover with the mantle of charity, the false opinions by which they undermine the gospel, to talk about the bitterness of controversy, (which they have provoked) to lament over divisions which they have made, and so if it were possible to deceive the very elect.

In the following, I think Mr. Cheeseman has presented his subject in a manner which appeals to the pious feelings, to the Christian emotions of every renewed heart. He may not have avoided all the severity which controversy engenders, but he has succeeded beyond my expectations in giving a practical character to the work. There is an application of the great principles of the gospel as he passes along, a flow of devotion, a kindling of the religious sensibilities, which must lead those who commence its perusal to the conclusion of the work. He makes the practical power of the doctrines of grace and redemption, so manifest, that the eyes of all unprejudiced persons can hardly fail to be opened, and if I mistake not, there will be left upon the mind of every reader, an impression of the importance of these great truths for which we stand in a day of darkness and rebuke.

DIFFERENCES BETWEEN
OLD AND NEW SCHOOL
PRESBYTERIANS.

CHAPTER I.

THE ECCLESIASTICAL DIFFERENCES BETWEEN OLD AND NEW SCHOOL PRESBYTERIANS.

The secession—Its causes—Changes in Church government and operations by the New School no improvement—Separation necessary to a reformation.

The divisions which exist between Old and New School Presbyterians, are calculated to produce any thing but pleasurable emotions in the bosoms of those who have been wont to pray for the peace of Jerusalem. And whatever can be done to unite in one body, those who are already united in their views of church government and of doctrinal and experimental religion, ought to be done by the friends of Zion.

The disowning act of 1837, has been extensively misunderstood. It has hitherto been represented, as an act by which four Synods were excommunicated for heresy, and that without a trial; when many individual ministers and churches and even whole Presbyteries, thus unjustly and summarily condemned, were sound in the faith. But when that act is carefully examined, it will be found that it excommunicated no one, and that it really separated no single Presbyterian minister or church from the General Assembly. While it disowned as unconstitutional, organizations compounded of Presbyterian and Congregational churches, it made provision for all who were truly Presbyterian, and gave them specific directions as to the course, which under their peculiar circumstances it was expedient for them to pursue. An act of dismemberment so suicidal as this is represented to have been, has no precedent in the history of the church. And while the desire of church extension remains so distinguishing an element in all denominational effort, it cannot be reasonably believed, that so large and respectable a body as the General Assembly of the Presbyterian Church, could so deliberately violate every principle of self love, and ecclesiastical policy, as is implied in this groundless imputation.

The subsequent secession of a large and respectable body of ministers and churches; the organization of a New General Assembly; their claim to be the Constitutional General Assembly; the suit at law instituted by them to obtain the name and the funds of the church, and its final decision against them, are events which belong to the history of past controversies and alienations, which, it is to be hoped, will never be renewed.

The act of 1837, cannot be believed to have been the cause of that secession. Had there existed no other causes, this isolated act, even though regarded as unconstitutional, would never have formed in the minds of reasonable men, a justifiable foundation for a course so extraordinary. Had there been no other causes in operation, the secession, it is believed, would never have taken place : but such causes were in operation. These causes had embarrassed the church for years in all her assemblies and in all her efforts. The secesion was not impulsive but deliberate; men had grown weary of debate, and had become chilled and alienated in their affections, by serious differences in ecclesiastical policy and in doctrinal and practical christianity. The bond that united them to the Presbyterian Church was not of the heart, and could not be, while they entertained views fundamentally at variance with her standards and her interests, and which brought them in perpetual conflict with their brethren. This frail bond, therefore, was easily cast off, and that without regret, and for a very insufficient ostensible reason. A new organization has been the result.

This new organization has termed itself triennial. It does not meet annually, as does the General Assembly of the Presbyterian Church, whose sessions have always been annual, and are found by long experience, not to be too frequent for a proper supervision of the churches, and for a vigorous and effective prosecution of the great work of education and missions. The seceders have at length discovered their error, and have endeavored to remedy it by annual conventions, and finally by an annual adjournment, which last step has involved them in controversy among themselves. While professing to improve by introducing a new order of things, they have found that change is not improvement.

Their assembly is not an appellate court; and the case of the Rev. Mr. Graham, who appeared before them for the redress of grievances, at their late meetings at Philadelphia and at Cincinnatti, has discovered the imbecility of a body, which could not do what it was so desirable and proper it should have done : it having formally abandoned so excellent a provision of the constitution. The man who ought to have had the judgment of the whole church in her collective wisdom on his case, was compelled, either to be condemned by one court, and justified by another of the same grade, or to abandon an organization which contained in itself the elements of its own dissolution.

The great head of the church has committed to her, in her organized capacity, the solemn and momentous work of evangelizing the world. "Out of Zion shall go forth the law, and the word of the Lord from Jerusalem. Go ye therefore, into all the world and preach the gospel to every creature." And the church can never cast off this obligation, by committing the high and sacred trust to voluntary associations, which have neither ecclesiastical existence or responsibility, and which are to take the whole work out of her hands and to do it for her. These views have been opposed by the New School, and they could not be satisfied until they had made experiments on a different plan.

The American Board, through which their charities have hitherto flowed, belongs no more to them than to us; and as they have no organizations of their own, and do next to nothing in their own appropriate capacity as a church of Jesus Christ to spread the gospel; and as they witness among themselves, a growing apathy on the subject of missions, and are feeling the fatal drain from surrounding and enterprising denominations, they are beginning to think soberly of a change, and will probably ere long, retract all they have ever said against ecclesiastical organizations.

The recent attack of some of their leading bodies on the American Tract Society, for mutilating the works of Dr. D' Aubigne, had no other origin in the judgment of many, than a desire to cover their retreat, and to create at once, organizations of their own. One of their leading men said to me not long since, "The Old School on this subject were right, and we were wrong." This opinion must ultimately prevail among them, or their growth and success is at an end. The American Board is falling back for support on the New England churches, where it originated and where it belongs.— The Presbyterian Church is increasing in her efforts and contributions, in a degree wholly unprecedented in any former period of her existence. Other denominations, by appealing to the just attachments of their own communicants to their own principles, are increasing in strength and effort; and unless the New School, abandon their position on this question, they will gradually weaken their own denominational bonds, and ultimately dissolve them altogether. Mutual affinities, social and religious, require to be cherished and strengthened by opening for them their natural and appropriate channel.

What, then, after a fair and unmolested experiment of ten

years? what great and good end has been attained by these various novelties in Presbyterianism? and what can we expect to gain by that other proposed novelty, an independent Synod in Western New York? If brethren are dissatisfied with their present connection with the Synod of Genesee, why do they not at once unite with the Synod of Buffalo? What call is there for covering this same field with a third fraction of the Presbyterian Church? If, as they affirm, they differ in no respect from the Old School body, but prefer it to all others, why not unite with it? They judge very incorrectly, if they regard the transition, which would be made by forming a union with a body to which the churches once belonged, and to which they now legitimately belong, as more abrupt than would be a transition to independency, a transition which with all their efforts, they have not been able to make, and which I am confident with an intimate acquaintance with all their plans and tendencies they never will make.

Neither will they ever join us in a body. If they wait for that period to arrive, they will always wait; if they ever resume their connection with our church, they will do it as others have done it: they will do it as individuals and as churches. Have the churches of the sixteenth century which fell off into Socinian error, yet returned to their former orthodoxy? Three hundred years is a long period to wait. Have the churches of Massachusetts, which fell into the Unitarian error, yet returned? Those who have waited there, are now conscious that they have waited too long, and are beginning to awake from their delusive dreams; and if these brethren wait until the Rochester Presbytery, or any other Presbytery in the Synod of Genesee, shall as a body correct its errors, abandon its Pelagianism, and resume its connection with the General Assembly, they *may* wait till their cold remains and mine shall moulder underneath the clods of the valley.

I do not contend for mere organizations. Organizations

can be of but little account except as they are a Scriptural means to an end; in this respect, some are greatly to be preferred above others. Among these the Presbyterian holds the first rank in our esteem, and Presbyterians should be the last to distrust or forsake it. It is valuable to me, not simply as it is an organization, but as it is authorized by the word of God, honored by his providence, blessed by the inhabitation of his spirit, and has always borne the testimony of Jesus.

When the minority of a body become unsound, there is no remedy but excision. When the majority become unsound, there is no remedy but secession. Error desires nothing, demands nothing but toleration. It is sure of ultimate success if let alone. Its advocates, to prevent alarm, maintain that the differences are but slight, perhaps merely verbal, or at most philosophical, and frown at suspicion and inquiry as calculated to disturb the peace of the church. They are the friends of union, but break up its foundations and "mine on in darkness." Error is more congenial than truth ; the love of it is the normal state, and its power of assimilation in this world is greater than that of truth. The gospel wins its way, and maintains its advantages against the current. Error floats with it, and gains its destination without lifting an oar. Truth in this world is an exotic. Error is indigenous. The former cannot live but by constant protection ; the latter thrives without it. Error, therefore, needs nothing but toleration in any communion, for its spread and success. The only successful preventative is excision or secession. To this rule there can be found no exception in the history of the past.

Our Lord when he appeared in Judea, found the Jews in a state of apostacy, and after a brief call to repentance and reformation, that people were abandoned to their fate, or rather, were excommunicated from the church of God. The decree is contained in the following statement ; " The kingdom of God shall be taken from you, and shall be given to a people bringing forth the fruits thereof." This is an example of high antiquity and of great authority, and every subsequent experiment has justified its wisdom.

The Church of Rome was long acknowledged by her friends to be in a state of alarming declension, and the efforts in favor of a reformation were numerous, wide-spread, and long continued. The celebrated Council of Constance assembled for no other end than to reform it ; yet that Council dissolved without effecting its object. The learned Erasmus sought the reformation of the Church of Rome as an end ; he condemned separation from it, he would not secede, but reform ; his whole life was wasted in worse then useless controversy, and he died at length disappointed and broken hearted. The early reformers sought at first a change in the church without a separation ; but they came to a better judgment in time to prevent another and a total failure. They acted upon the model left them by their Lord, and their success began with their imitation of that model : with their total separation from the Church of Rome.

Organizations give to principles a formal existence, and bring them at once within the range of a possible propagation and succession. But without them they are as spirits without bodies ; they awaken no sympathies among men ; they are not felt, because they are not known ; they have no general and permanent visibility, and therefore can exert no general and permanent influence. Whitefield visited this country and labored with unexampled popularity and success ; yet he has left no permanent imprint of his opinions on the character of the American people. They expired with his personal ministry, because he gave them no existence in an organization. Wesley, who appeared here at the same time, was far more provident, and gave to his opinions a permanent home in the bosom of an organization ; and though his voice is no more heard, his venerable form no more seen among his followers, yet he continues to direct their labors, and to fix and control their sentiments. Dr. Witherspoon engaged in an effort to reform the Church of Scotland, but gave up in despair, and came to America. He united with our body, and preached the sermon at the organization of the General Assembly in 1789. Reform measures have more or less existed since his day, in the Kirk which he felt it his duty to abandon; and during the last twenty years, the controversy has received new life from the opposition made to the godly and earnest endeavor after a thorough reformation. The middle party took their usual position between truth and error, and became the most efficient supporters of the latter. Dr. Witherspoon's ecclesiastical characteristics are as descriptive now, as they were ninety years ago of these moderate, no-party men, who become "fierce for moderation." The sound portion of the church, however, have after a long and failing struggle, at length resorted to the true and only remedy, *separation;* and by this movement have put themselves in the way of the most wonderful reformation in modern times. United with the Kirk, they were the Nazarite shorn of his locks; separated from it, the pillars of Erastianism already quake at their approach.

The necessity and utility of an organization, under our own control, to contain and to continue our doctrines, is urged upon us then, by the entire experience and wisdom of the past. Those Presbyterians, who remain in the New School organization to reform it, or who unite with it from our body for that purpose, are worse than dead to us, and to the cause of reform. Neither their wisdom nor power to manage and control unsound bodies, can be believed to surpass all those who have gone before them, and who have invariably failed in the same effort. It is useless to urge that the present case is an exception to the rule; it has not proved itself an exception hitherto, and it never will. Those therefore, who fall into the snare of these abortive policies, need no prophet to assure them of the inevitable result.

It must be painful, also, to occupy a false position, to disguise our real designs, and to practice on a confidence which would be withheld at once from us if we were thoroughly understood, if we were as transparent as we ought to be, if we were "an epistle known and read of all men." Services so equivocal, not to say disreputable and sinful, are not required of the "children of the light and of the day," and though they may acquire a temporary popularity, they must end in shame. There is withal a most undesirable habit formed, under circumstances so unfavorable to the culture and exercise of candor and integrity. We become practiced in the low arts of cunning, deception, and management, and weaken and destroy a most lovely trait in Christian character. But aside from the impropriety of the course itself, in its own nature, no enlightened friend of our church can pursue it long, with an honest design to benefit our cause; for he places himself at once in opposition to it by his *position*, his *efforts*, and his *influence*.

His *position* is that of an antagonist.

His *efforts* weaken our existing organizations, by drawing from them our ministers and members. They become necessary to his success, his most reliable auxiliaries in his revolutionary movement; and, should he find us on the alert, and unable to appreciate either his wisdom or his ill-advised friendship—if he do not at length become restive, and give us hard names, and prejudice our cause in the very quarter in which he went to strengthen it, he will prove the first exception with which I have ever met. I know no one as yet who has been captivated by these ambiguous policies, who has not ultimately been ensnared in this manner, and done more to alienate our friends, weaken our cause, and provoke opposition, than those who were always open and avowed in their enmities.

Those also who are retained in an unsound connection by this *influence* will remain there from the same cause; and their names, their property, and their offspring, will be lost to our church. In a few more years, the present incumbents of these pulpits will be no more ; and however useful they may have been in their personal ministry, they cannot control the succession. That is in other hands, and will be much more likely to take its complexion from the living than from the dead ; from the body in which they have left their churches, than from the pastor's remembered wishes.*

In whatever light, then, this policy is examined, whether with reference to the past or the present, its character or tendency, it but strengthens our position—that the true remedy against error, is the maintainance of the gospel in separate organizations ; and that the expectation of success, in any other way, will invariably end in disappointment.

The churches here have listened to one side of the question, only. We never have been permitted to plead our cause before them, and many of them, therefore, are made to believe themselves to be in the very body by which they were originally organized. Did they know that they were not ; that they had been kept in the dark by interested individuals ; had, without a full and sufficient examination of the question, without a fair and impartial presentation of it in all its aspects, been drawn off into a new organization ; an organization scarcely ten years old ; an organization changed in its forms, and changed in its doctrines ; there are many

---

* I little expected when this was penned, that before it would be in type, my best friend, and most reliable counselor, the Rev. NORRIS BULL, D. D. would be no more. His piety, integrity, perseverance, skill, and courage ; his great intellectual endowments, and his remarkable power over deliberative assemblies, qualified him preeminently for success in the difficult circumstances in which he was placed. All eyes were turned toward him as the leader of a forlorn hope in the Synod of Genesee. And when one by one his friends forsook him, because they deemed the contest in which he was engaged, hopeless, and yet saw him almost alone and with unbroken resolution, still battling with his destiny, they could not but admire, and sometimes hope for partial success from his singular perseverence. But now that he rests from his labors, every expectation of reforming even a single Presbytery, is buried with him.

decided Presbyterians who would not long remain where they are, but would avail themselves of the earliest favorable opportunity of carrying out the provisions of the act of 1837, and would resume their connection with our church.

I know men who tremble in their places lest the truth should be known on this subject, whose whole efforts are directed to suppress inquiry by scandalous imputations, or by bringing up false issues, and who look upon a fair discussion as calculated to benefit any but themselves. If, however, our cause is to be defended by such weapons, it shall not be by our hands. It is of God, and it will stand. If it is not of Him, let it perish ; it is not worth preserving.

CHAPTER II.

DOCTRINAL DIFFERENCES BETWEEN OLD AND NEW SCHOOL PRESBYTERIANS.

Sufferings of Christ—The New School deny their penal nature—They were penal.

The published works of leading divines, give character to their respective communions. The published works of Arius and Arminius, not the creeds which they respectively subscribed, and which were sufficiently sound, but their own expositions of their creed, are the sources to which we resort to ascertain their opinions and those of their followers. And in like manner, not the creed alone of the New School body, but their explanations of that creed as contained in the widely circulated writings of their leading and influential divines, are another and an ultimate criterion, to which we must resort to ascertain what is really their denominational theology. To shrink from this most reasonable test, or to attempt to evade it by denying its correctness, is not only suspicious, but prima facie evidence of conscious weakness and guilt. It is in effect to resolve society into its original and independent elements, and to destroy the very principle of associated responsibility.

The declaration of independency on the part of the Rochester Presbytery, so long as it is a mere declaration, can form no exception in their favor. If it had been carried out; if they had broken connection with the New School body, and formed an organization under their own control, they would have secured our confidence. But for them to affirm that they are independent, and not responsible for the New School errors, and at the same time to remain as they do in the New School connection, is, to say the softest thing we can of it, disingenuous and calculated to deceive. Were not the members of the Rochester Presbytery generally present at the late session of their Synod, and did they not hear the Moderator,* in his Synodical Sermon, distinctly, solemnly, and with emphasis, declare that " Jesus Christ did not suffer the penalty of the law nor any part of it ?" And what has that Presbytery done, and what has that Synod done, to rebuke this bold denial of the Gospel? And can these brethren be ignorant of the tolerated Pelagian and Socinian errors which infest the whole body? Surely the claim to orthodoxy and independency under such circumstances, is a claim which few can respect but themselves. If I could possibly understand their position as they appear to understand it, I should be happy to make an exception in their favor ; but as it is, they must be held to the proposed test in common with the rest of their brethren.

Dr. Beman, whose work on the Atonement, is hailed by the last Moderator of the New School General Assembly, Dr. Cox, " with devout salutation, commendation, and benediction," maintains that Christ did not endure the penalty of the law ; that his sufferings were in no sense penal ; whereas the Scriptures affirm that the " chastisement or punishment of our peace was upon Him ;" that the " Lord did lay upon Him the iniquity of us all ;" Isaiah 53.—and that " Christ has redeemed us from the curse of the law, being made a curse for us." Galatians iii. 13.

" That Jesus Christ did not die in the strict and literal sense, as the substitute of His people, or in the room of those

---

* Rev. Wm. F. Curry.

who will finally be saved, may be established beyond all reasonable doubt—beyond all enlightened controversy." * * *
" The law can have no penal demand except against the offender. With a substitute it has no concern ; and though a thousand substitutes should die, the law in itself considered, and left to its own natural operation, would have the same demand on the transgressor which it always had. This claim can never be invalidated. This penal demand can never be extinguished." * * * * " The penalty of the law, strictly speaking, was not inflicted at all." * * * * " The whole legal system has been suspended, at least, for the present, in order to make way for the operation of one of a different character." (Dr. Beman on Atonement, pp. 96. 133.) Whereas, the Scriptures affirm that it is not suspended at all ; that " till Heaven and earth pass away, one jot or one tittle shall in no wise pass from the law, till all be fulfilled ;" Math. v. 18.—and that Christ who " was made sin for us who knew no sin, that we might be made the righteousness of God in Him ;" 2. Cor. v. 21.—" is the end of the law for righteousness to every one that believeth." Rom. x. 4. " He hath magnified the law and made it honorable." Isa. xlii. 21.

Dr. Beman can see no point in Dr. Priestley's objections against the doctrine of atonement, as against his own views, for he fully agrees with Dr. Priestly, that there could be no mercy in acquitting the guilty, when justice had already been fully satisfied by a substitute. (See Beman on the Atonement, p. 138.)

The error of Dr. Beman, and his Unitarian friend, must be obvious to the most ordinary capacity. It assumes that satisfaction, even though it proceed from the offended party himself, would be no exhibition of mercy to the offender. If this satisfaction, however, had been made by some being extraneous to the law giver, the objection might have force, but proceeding as it does from the bosom of the ever-blessed God himself, who both finds and gives the ransom, and who in His infinite pity does not spare His own Son; the objection is unscriptural, and rests upon a false assumption. If a friend of an insolvent debtor, were to satisfy the firm to which he was indebted, their release of him, would not be an act of mercy, but of justice. But if the partners of that firm were themselves, by paying their equal proportions, to liquidate the claim against him, it would give a new aspect to the whole affair, and it would be idle to say that there was no mercy shown towards him by his creditors in thus themselves satisfying the claims of the firm. Satisfaction, therefore, to the justice of God, does not determine the question whether mercy is exercised or not in the sinner's pardon. That is to be determined by another and distinct inquiry, viz: Who rendered that satisfaction? The answer is, "God so loved the world, that He gave his only begotten Son that whosoever believeth on Him should not perish, but have everlasting life." John iii. 16.

The notes of Mr. Barnes are extensively circulated, and have supplanted Henry, Scott, and the Catechism, in all the Bible classes and Sabbath schools here. They load the shelves of our book stores, and have become the pocket companions of religious teachers in the New School body. Mr. Barnes does more to form the religious opinions and characters of the rising generation among them, than all their ministers collectively. He is more cautious than Dr. Beman; more skilled in indirection and circumlocution; there is a blandness and sanctity in his manner that puts you off your guard when you read him; his blows are more in the dark, and then he says so many kind things afterwards, and makes so many concessions, you can hardly believe it was he. But still, after a careful and thorough examination, I am prepared to say, that Mr. Barnes and Dr. Beman teach the same doctrine on the subject of the atonement.

On 2 Cor. v. 21, " He hath made him *to be* sin for us." In

his third inquiry, his language is, "Can it mean that he was, in any proper sense of the word, guilty? For no one is truly guilty who is not personally a transgressor of the law; and if he was in any proper sense guilty, then he deserved to die, and his death could have no more merit than that of any other guilty being; and if he was properly guilty, it would make no difference in this respect whether it was by his own fault or by imputation." Again, on Gal. iii. 13:— "Christ has redeemed us from the curse of the law, being made a curse for us." In his fourth remark, he declares that, "It cannot be meant that the Lord Jesus properly bore the penalty of the law; His sufferings were in the place of the penalty, not the penalty itself." And in his notes on Isai. liii. 5: "The chastisement of our peace was upon Him." (After stating that the word, chastisement, does not of necessity denote punishment, though he admits that it is frequently used in that sense,) he declares that "here it cannot properly mean punishment;" and thus, on every proof text on this subject, he evades and denies the usual interpretation, and gives another. If he has any skill as a polemic, any knowledge of the original Greek or Hebrew, whatever he has of learning or of skill, it is brought to bear against these time hallowed turrets of an orthodox faith. While he professes not to write for the critical, but for the common reader, he puts forth all his strength on these passages, and leaves not a single expedient untried to dissatisfy us with the usual interpretation. That interpretation is never correctly given, or given as it would have been by a Presbyterian. And finally, we are told that whatever else the passage may mean, it does not teach the doctrine contended for from it.

Take one instance, among many, to illustrate his tact at indirection. On Rom. viii. 7: "Because the carnal mind is enmity against God: for it is not subject to the law of God, neither indeed can be." He states that "the apostle does not express any opinion about the metaphysical ability of man, or discuss that question at all." Again: "The affirmation does not mean that the heart of the sinner might not be subject to God, or that his soul is so physically depraved that he cannot obey, or that he might not obey the law. On that subject the Apostle here expresses no opinion; that is not the subject of discussion." Here we are told substantially, that the very thing which the Apostle did say, he did not say, or at least that he did not mean to say it; yea, that he expressed no opinion on that point, selecting the very point on which the Apostle expresses himself in the most decided terms, and contriving to contradict him without seeming to do so, and that by an adroit introduction of the words metaphysical and physical. But with all that singular evasiveness which pervades his whole manner, he obviously agrees with the New School on every material question.

I need not pause here to show that these views of the death of Christ, are Unitarian, not Presbyterian; that they are the former, and not the latter, is quite certain.* But the great objection to them, is, that they are not scriptural.—Presbyterianism is nothing to me as it is Presbyterianism, but as it is the gospel, as it contains, and exhibits and defends *it*, in that respect, it is to me everything. Were not the matters at issue between us, of the most serious nature, if these errors were not mining at the very foundations of our hopes for eternity, I should not have adventured before you in this form. Not to be tenacious of peculiarities, to be yielding and pliant in all that does not interfere with truth and righteousness, is a lovely trait in christian character, a grace which should be sedulously cultivated, that we may be both more agreeable and useful; but carried too far, we may, and often do, mar where we intend to beautify, and ruin, when we intend to save. Influenced by these considerations, I

---

* Christ "felt and bore the weight of God's wrath." Lar. Cat. Ans. 40. "Endured most grevious torments immediately in his soul." Con. of Faith, chap. viii: sec. 4.

cannot pass these bold denials of Bible truth, without indulging in further animadversions ; without attempting to send the antidote with the poison.

What proof has Dr. Beman given beyond his own assertion, " That the penalty of the law was not inflicted at all ?" or Mr. Barnes, "that if Christ were properly guilty by imputation, his death could have no more merit than that of any other guilty being?" These are naked assertions, wholly unsupported by the word of God, and I have not yet, in all they have said, met with a single attempt formally to prove them from the scriptures by the quotation of a solitary passage containing such an idea. Indeed, the scriptures contain no such statements, but throughout present the opposite view. Hence the controversy between us and the New School, resembles that with the Universalists. We bring direct proof texts. They bring none. We attack. They parry. We bring the witnesses. They assail them. The Bible never brought their system a single shred to cover its nakedness ; it is in their way, and involves them at once, and at every step, in a debate with its obvious meaning. Oh ! what a contrast is there between the two following statements :—" Christ hath redeemed us from the curse of the law, being made a curse for us." Gal. iii. 13. " The penalty of the law, strictly speaking, was not inflicted at all." Beman on Atonement, p. 133. And how weak and repulsive the following abortive attempt to obscure and pervert the obvious meaning of this text : "Cursed is every one that hangeth on a tree." "Does the law say the soul that sinneth it shall—hang on a tree—It is a curse, but not the curse of the law." Beman on Atonement, p. 112. Yes, truly it was a curse. His death by the civil law was penal. "If he had not been a malefactor," said his accusers, " we would not have delivered him to thee." He was judged worthy of death, and that death was a judicial infliction. The passage in Deut. xxi. 22, 23, here referred to, is not cited by Paul, to prove that Christ endured the penalty of the civil, but of the divine law. Hence, the apostle selects that part of it which relates exclusively to the latter, and not to the former, to wit : "He that hangeth on a tree is accursed of God." He was suspended between heaven and earth ; he was not admitted to either, he was excluded from both. While his being lifted up, expressed as a a symbolic action, the ignominious light in which he was viewed and treated by the court on earth ; it also expressed with equal significance, the ignominious light in which he was viewed and treated by the court in Heaven. But the ignominy of hanging on the tree, was too great an honor for one who was "accursed of God." He must not hang all night upon the tree. That were "an eye-sore for heaven to look upon." God was now become party to the quarrel against his life, and the wretch must be hid at once in the earth. "Thou shalt in any wise bury him the same day." In Gal. iii. 13, the discussion is of the divine law, whose terrific curse pealed in thunder from the burning mountain, and the passage cited is in proof that Christ endured it. His hanging on a tree is the public evidence and manifestation of the penal nature of His sufferings under the divine law, to wit : that he was "accursed of God." The manner of his death was previously and deliberately arranged, that the evidence of its nature might be full, public and conclusive. It was "by the determinate counsel and fore-knowledge of God." Acts ii. 23. And it was by the concurrence and choice of Jesus Christ. Of his life he says, "I lay it down of myself." John x. 18. Except for the evidence that his hanging on a tree would furnish of the nature of the transaction, his death could as well have been by the axe, or by strangulation, as by the tree. But the manner of his death, together with the supernatural earthquake, the strange commotion in the grave yard, the midnight darkness that gathered on the face of the frowning heavens, the confession of the Centurion, and the remorseful gesture of all who came together to that sight—mingled their testimony with the expiring groans of the Son of God, and called the attention of every intelligence in heaven, earth and hell, to the tree, to the public evidence of a penal infliction, to the horror, despair and woe of Him who was "the accursed of God." And yet Dr. Beman can discover no evidence, that the sufferings of Christ were penal, even from the highest possible evidence which could be afforded him of that fact. And his denial of it is too gross a contradiction of the word of God; too gross a violation of all the principles of correct and satisfactory interpretation, to challenge either respect or confidence.— His assertion that the penalty of the law was "immensely another kind of death in form, duration and circumstances;" "that the penalty of the law was damnation, or eternal death," is a puerility unworthy of a grave and learned divine. The damned have not suffered eternally, and yet their sufferings are penal, and their entrance upon their final state, by death, whether by violence or by lingering disease, is the hopeless commencement of them. Every lost sinner also suffers according to the deeds done in the body ; but these deeds are not the same in number or aggravation. The suffering must, therefore, vary in every instance. Fallen angels, also, who have no bodies, do not suffer precisely in the same manner as do those who are "cast both soul and body into hell." Math. x. 28. The penalty is death, and that must adapt itself to the nature and dignity of the being on whom it falls. Creatures can never remove their obligations to endure it because they are finite. The eternity of their woe is incidental; i. e., it arises not from the law, but from their natures. The duration of the suffering is not necessary to the proper infliction of the penalty, (by whomsoever endured,) but necessary to it when endured by creatures. But the Son of God was not a creature, and could exhaust a penalty in a limited period, which a creature could never exhaust. It assailed him, and bruised his body, and bore him down to the very gates of hell; but his divinity consumed its strength, and bore it back, and broke the arm of its power. It cried out for blood! its cry was remorseless and unceasing. Along the flight of weary centuries, it had made the place of worship the place of continued slaughter; it had forever wasted the precious life, and still had demanded blood. It could not be satisfied with the blood of beasts, it also kindled on the souls of men, drank up their spirits, and burned, and burned forever. But when it reached the Son of God, its rage was spent; its triumphs ended; its power destroyed. It could not long grapple for the mastery with an uncreated arm; it kindled fiercely on his humanity, and wasted it; it burned towards his divinity, and expired. Death simply considered, is not necessarily the penalty of the law, as the death of plants and animals. The penal nature of the infliction is to be determined from the grounds and reasons of it; not wholly from its "form, duration, and circumstances," but, also, and mainly, from the judgment and design of the court in pronouncing the sentence, and the actual execution of the culprit in pursuance of that judgment. Christ was adjudged to death by the Father for our sins. "He hath made him to be sin for us." 2 Cor. v. 21. And that judgment was executed both by his providence and by his agency. "It pleased the Lord to bruise him." "Thou hast put him to grief." Isaiah liii. "He was delivered for our offences." Rom. iv. 25. In every scriptural explanation of the death of Christ is invariably included the punishment of sin.

The attempts of the New School in any other way to prove that Christ did not suffer penally, are equally a failure. It is not a question of reason, but of revelation, and above the reach of mere reason. The moment they leave the Bible, the proofs which would be required, lie beyond the vision of men and of angels. "Canst thou by searching find out God? Canst thou find out the Almighty unto perfection?

It is high as heaven; what canst thou do? deep as hell; what canst thou know?" There is "a more sure word of prophesy; ** a light that shineth in a dark place," to which we do well to take heed; and to abandon it, is not to multiply the facilities for correct and satisfactory investigation, but to be left "alone, at midnight, on a dark and moonless sea." Who can show, and by what process of reasoning, that God the Father and the Son, could not so transfer the obligation to suffer the penalty of the law for the sins of his people to Jesus Christ, as to make those sufferings really penal, in the judgment of Him whose judgment is according to truth? What though we grant, for the sake of the argument, that all analogy fails us here? The same is true of the incarnation. And it is not a question of analogy, but of revelation, in a matter with which analogy can have but little to do, when we have once forsaken the Scriptures and their analogies. We are, in that event, borne by it beyond where "eye can see or glass can reach," to scan the ways of Him, "whose ways are not as our ways, and whose thoughts are not as our thoughts," whose purposes are hid from us in the midnight of eternity, where roll the clouds of an appalling darkness, and where mysterious thunders utter their voices. How, then, *can* we, having left the Bible testimony—to examine in the abstract what it is possible for God to do—how *can* we, how dare any mortal say, that "If Christ were properly guilty by imputation, he deserved to die; and [that] his death could have no more merit than that of any other guilty being?"

These objections of the New School, against the penal nature of Christ's sufferings, are not scriptural, but philosophical. And the philosophy is obviously false, because it assumes what cannot be proved, and because it flatly contradicts the analogical and the direct testimony of the word of God. The innocent invariably suffered in the place of the guilty under the law of Moses; the whole proceeding was upon legal principles; and it is abundantly and directly affirmed, that Christ suffered on legal principles. The Son had power over his own life, and for the all-sufficient reason which the Scriptures assign: He was God. As such, he was not subject, necessarily, to those rules in the regulation of his conduct, which must bind and govern the creature. As a condition of nature would exempt angels from the obligations which govern us in our domestic relations, so the Son of God is exempted, by his infinite deity, in disposing of his own life, from the obligations imposed upon all others. I understand our Lord to convey this idea, when he says: "No man taketh my life from me, but I lay it down of myself. I have power to lay it down, and I have power to take it again." John x. 18. He frequently asserts his absolute power and unbounded mastery over life and death. "I am the first and the last; I am he that liveth and was dead; and behold, I am alive for evermore, Amen; and have the keys of hell and of death." Rev. i. 17, 18.

What is true of the Son, is equally true of the Father; and for the same reasons: *He is God.* This is the ultimate ground of all obligation; the ultimate reason given by him for all his commandments, and for all his wonderful and mysterious dispensations. It is appended to all the covenants, and throughout the old and new Testaments, is the high and ultimate warrant for every rite and every institution. God said unto Moses, say unto the Children of Israel, "Thus saith the Lord." If his commission was challenged, he was to prove its divinity by miracles; but still to insist on this one ultimate ground of obligation, submission and obedience: "Thus saith the Lord." God, then, as the Governor of the Universe, could do what no human government could, because he had in reserve vast and incomprehensibly great and glorious prerogatives; prerogatives which he would never give to another, and in the exercise of which he accepted the obedience and death of his Son, voluntarily offered, and inflicted upon him the punishment due to the sins of his people. It is, therefore, because he is God, and not man, that we are not consumed. This is not only true with respect to his compassion, but also with respect to those inexhaustible resources in his own blessed nature, for its constant and sufficient development and exercise. He is God; God in three persons; God above all law; and, therefore, able to obey it; to satisfy its claims; to inflict its curse; to deliver from it; and to shed unbounded glory on the institution of his justice, while he justifies the trembling believer in Jesus.

The right which a man might have to give up his own life, in the place of that of his friend, in order to satisfy the civil law; and the right which any earthly tribunal might have to accept the substitution, are both highly questionable; because neither of the parties have any authority, other than that which is derivative. That the proceeding might be made perfectly clear and satisfactory, they would be required to show that they possessed an original and underived right to act in the premises, or, at least, a warrant from God, the original fountain of all law and justice. And as men, respected as individuals, or as associated under conventional laws, do not possess the one, and cannot produce the other, so the right, by consent of parties, to substitute the innocent for the guilty, in the inflictions of criminal justice, does not appear obvious. But, this cannot be true of the high contracting parties in the sacrifice of atonement. Both possessed a right, which was original and underived. The infinite God is not to be circumscribed and chained within narrow limits, as though he were a creature of yesterday. Human laws, and the right to administer them, are grants, adequate to the necessities of our present state, and limited by the divine will; but the source of all justice is infinitely free, and He hath done whatever pleased Him, and gives us the highest possible reasons for his conduct, when he assures us, that it "seemed good in his sight." As time is a point thrown from the cycles of eternity, to be speedily absorbed and lost in its source, so human governments are appointed to answer their temporary end, and pass away, or be lost in their source, that "God may be all in all." Christ, then, we maintain, was made a curse for us, and it was possible for God to do what he in fact did, when he inflicted upon him the punishment of our peace. Christ was the master of life, and had an original and underived power over his own life, in a sense in which it could not be true of any created intelligence. He had a right to lay it down in blood, for the sins of his people, to the justice of the Father, and to resume it again at his pleasure. This right he also exercised, when he "made his soul an offering for sin."

The crucifixion of the Son of God is seen and felt by all, to have been an event unparalleled in the records of martyrdom. And when its penal nature has been denied, the demand for some other plausible explanation has been felt to be imperious. Hence writers of this class have dwelt largely on its moral influence. "He stood (says Mr. Barnes) in the centre of the universe, the sun grew dark, and the dead arose, and angels gazed upon the scene, and from his cross an impression went abroad to the fartherest part of the universe." Notes Gal. ii. 16. "We may very naturally suppose that it was the design, or purpose of God, in saving sinners, to make a deep aud grand impression on the universe." See Beman on Atonement, p. 42. The Unitarians seek relief for their system in the same way. "The cross (says Dr. Dewey) sets a darker stamp upon the malignity of sin, than the table of the commandments; and it demands of us, in accents louder than Sinai's thunder, sympathetic agonies to be freed from sin." Controversial Discourses, p. 82. The moral influence of the sufferings of Christ, on the whole intelligent universe, we believe to be inconceivably great and glorious, because they are seen and felt to be the righteous inflictions of legal justice. The angels, who kept not their first estate, are "set forth for an example, suffering the vengeance of eternal fire." Jude, vi. 7. The suffering is not just, because it is impressive, but impressive, because it is just. And if Christ's sufferings, were not merited by the sins of his people, which were set to his account; if he did not suffer, "the just for the unjust; (1st Peter, iii. 18.;) if he was not "bruised for our iniquities," (Isa. lv. 5.,) then there could arise out of them no desirable moral influence whatever. If God did not "make him to be sin for us," (2d Cor. v. 21.,) how could his sufferings impress us with the evil of sin? For "who ever perished, being innocent?" Job, iv. 7. And what good could come of it, if any ever had; if such foul wrong had ever been perpetrated by the ever blessed God? Could it "please the Lord to bruise him, and put his soul to grief," to administer the cup of trembling in the garden, to smite the Shepherd, and forsake him on the cross? when justice had no claims to vindicate, the law no demands to satisfy? And could the holy universe behold the fearful spectacle, without a thrill of horror and despair?

This attempted explanation is no explanation. It encumbers the system with additional dfficulties, and leaves its advocates to grapple with an objection which they can never remove. The restraining moral influence of the death of Christ is not with us its principle, but rather we would say, its incidental end. Christ did far more than impress the universe with the evil of sin. He did all "for man" or in his place, that needed to be done "in things pertaining to God," whose justice, was the great obstacle in the way of salvation. The innocent need no substitute : no one to represent them. Their communications with God are always acceptable and direct. "I am Gabriel, that stand in the presence of God," he stands there, without a mediator, because he is not an offender. But we are guilty; are his banished ones, and can no longer act for ourselves, in those high and holy things that respect the justice of God. In this great work, impossible to be done by a sinner or a creature, the Son of God stands alone, in solitary greatness, sharing his sacerdotal work and glory, with no other. All the significancies of the priestly office were in the high priest. He alone represented Christ, and went alone into the most holy place to make atonement for sin. And Christ stood alone, and of the people there was none with him. He went alone into the mountain, to be tempted, " to distrust, devil-worship, and self-murder." He was not supported in his agony in the garden, by his disciples : they could not watch one hour. He stood alone in Pilate's judgment hall, abandoned by all, defended by none. He hung alone on the cross, derided by thieves, and forsaken of God. He descended alone into the grave, pursuing the last enemy and vanquishing him, single handed, in his last and gloomy retreat. And if he has left anything undone, that needed to have been done, that unfinished work, can be finished by no other. If he has not done *all*, the fate of his church, would be the same as though he had done *nothing*. If then, among all the great things he has accomplished, he has omitted to bear the penalty of the law, if it never has been inflicted at all on him, its infliction must inevitably fall upon his ruined people, and they must sink to hell for "God will by no means clear the guilty." Exodus xxxiv. 7. "He abideth faithful; he cannot deny himself." 2 Tim. ii. 13. But he has not omitted to bear it, neither has the Father omitted to inflict it. for "It pleased the Lord to bruise him." "Thou hast put him to grief." "He made his soul an offering for sin." On these passages in the 53d of Isaiah, Mr. Barnes has bestowed much learned labor, to no good purpose. They mean more, than that Christ was delivered up to outward providential sufferings; they represent those sufferings, to have also proceeded from the Father in direct and subjective inflictions. This, it is true, would prove them penal; and they were such. This, which is the common interpretation, and the manifest sense of the words of the prophet, receives collateral support also, from the narrative given of the wonderful event. His courage and fortitude, his personal purity and peace of conscience, and every other element of greatness and glory, that ever entered into the nature or adorned the character of man, stood pre-eminent in him, and placed him above all others. But when did ever martyr, spend a night of gloom and despair and bloody agony, comparable with that, in which Jesus was betrayed? Paul sang at midnight, when his back was sore with stripes, and his feet made fast in the stocks. He remained unmoved amid bonds and afflictions, and was ready to be offered up, and cheerful in the immediate prospect of a violent death. But Christ was "sore amazed and being in agony, sweat as it were great drops of blood falling down to the ground." It was not the mere dread of whips and thorns, of treason and crucifixion, that could have had power to baptize in blood, one so truly great and good. There were other and higher causes in operation, and to these he repeatedly refers. When the bitter cup was pressed to his fevered lip, it was seen and acknowledged by him to have been administered by the Father's hand; and though he prayed that it might pass, yet he submitted to him who would not suffer it to pass; for the cup which his heavenly father gave him to drink, should he not drink it? There are no out cries, when he is scourged, and crowned with thorns, and nailed to the cross; during this entire period of intense bodily pain, "he opened not his mouth." But when at length, it pleased the Lord again to bruise him; when God himself drew the sword, and again directly smote the shepherd; then a loud and plaintive voice, wails out mournfully from the cross: "Why hast thou forsaken me?" Mat. xxvii. 46. It is an expostulation not with man but with God, and directs our attention to the source of his woe, and helps to finish and explain, the mournful tragedy recorded by the prophet Isaiah. May this bitter curse never fall on us, for who can abide it? Who can dwell in devouring fire. Who can dwell with everlasting burnings? Isa. xxxiii. 14. Inflicted on Christ, it could not last; it approached his divinity, and perished from the way. Inflicted on creatures, it must last forever; empty upon their devoted heads the vials of its wrath: a wretchedness, concentrated and interminable. O! how gloomy and hopeless that prison, in which it confines the final enemies of God. The walls are never scaled, the bolts are never drawn, the horrors never end. Who then can abide it? Fall somewhere, it must; if you neglect Christ and die in your sins; it will claim you for its prey, drink up your spirits, soak like oil into your bones, and fill you with an intense misery, like to that which sore amazed the son of God, and pressed him to the ground, and moistened the weeping turf with his blood. It exhausted itself on him: He was divine. It never will on the lost: They are creatures. "Their worm dieth not, their fire is not quenched." Mark ix. 44. Are you yet in your sins? escape to him at once, for how shall we escape if we neglect so great salvation. As a Saviour, he stands alone, and of the people there are none with him; there is no other eye to pity, no other arm to save. Neglect him, and whatever else you may do, to whomsoever else you may go, you cannot escape; you must bear the curse yourself. It is not sufficient to regard him as a good man, as a suffering martyr, nor even as divine. If his sufferings were but an expedient, or any thing else whatever you may be pleased to make them, and yet not the curse of the law, you err on the main point: and as his satisfaction can benefit you only as it is accepted, it cannot benefit you in respect of the curse, for that you believe was not endured by him. He cannot then save you from it, and how can you escape? Your error here is most fatal. If you believe that God can safely and with honor give up the curse, since Christ has suffered, though he did not suffer *it,* yet that faith cannot save you: God is true and just and "cannot deny himself." 2. Timothy ii. 13. He will inflict the curse. And if the Saviour has not borne, he cannot bring you out from under it. It must in that event abide on you forever. And can you abide it? O! turn not away from him who hung upon the tree, with this ruinous evasion of his proffered grace. "He that believeth on the Son hath everlasting life, but he that believeth not the Son, shall not see life but the wrath of God abideth on him." John iii. 36. Or can you have a heart thus to slight the grace of Him, who in his infinite pity, took your place under the broken covenant. An interest in this wonderful event is felt every where else. Hell is moved from beneath and, devils cry, "we know thee, who thou art;" angels bow from their bright principalities, in the heavenly places and "desire to look into the mysteries of his love;" the vail of the temple is rent in twain from top to bottom; the earth quakes; the dead arise; the rocks cry out; and can you, you who are most of all concerned—can you remain unmoved amid the awakened sympathies of surrounding worlds? Oh! what is this which has thus availed "to harden all within?" Is not such depravity total? Shall the scene on calvary affect the universe and break the very heart of marble, and wilt thou shed no tear, nor treat even with common decency the overtures of grace?

> "I asked the heavens,—" What foe to God hath done
> This unexampled deed?—The heavens exclaim,
> "'Twas man! and we in horror, snatch'd the sun
> From such a spectacle of guilt and shame."
> I asked the sea;—the sea in fury boil'd,
> And answerd with his voice of storms, 'twas man!
> My waves in panic, at his crime recoil'd,
> Disclosed th' abyss, and from the centre ran.
> I ask'd the earth;—the earth replied aghast,
> "'Twas man!—and such strange pangs my bosom rent,
> That still I groan and shudder at the past."
> —To man, gay, smiling, thoughtless man, I went,
> And asked him next:—*He* turn'd a scornful eye,
> Shook his proud head, and deigned me no reply."

CHAPTER III.

DOCTRINAL DIFFERENCES CONTINUED.

Imputation—What intended by it—Denied by the New School—The doctrine defended—New School views of faith exposed and refuted.

The doctrine of Imputation, is distinctly taught in the word of God. " To him that worketh not, but believeth on him that justifieth the ungodly, his faith is counted to him, for righteousness: even as David, also, describeth the blessedness of the man, unto whom God imputeth righteousness, without works." Romans iv. 5, 6. In this passage God is said to account a man legally just, who is not so in fact.— He justifieth the ungodly. The term, justifieth, is forensic. It relates to the judgment of a court, in the case of an accused person, who is pronounced just according to the law. But in this instance the person justified, is confessedly ungodly, he is counted to be in law, what he is not in fact, and this by imputation. God imputes to him righteousness without works. This righteousness is a reality. He does not impute to him what does not exist. And if it does not exist in the person justified, it must exist somewhere else. To impute a nonentity is both absurd and impossible. This righteousness was wrought out by the obedience of Jesus Christ. " By the obedience of one, shall many be made righteous." Romans v. 19. The son "was made under the law, to redeem them that were under the law." Galatians iv. 4, 5. " He became obedient unto death." Phil. ii. 8.

"Fulfilled all righteousness." Mat. iii. 15. "And is the end of the law for righteousness to every one that believeth." Romans x. 4. This righteousness is called the righteousness of God. "Therein (in the gospel) is the righteousness of God revealed," Romans i. 17—not his " method, or plan," as Mr. Barnes will have it, but his righteousness. It is called *the righteousness of God*, because wrought out by God the Son, brought savingly to the knowledge of the believer by God the Holy Ghost, and provided and imputed by God the Father.

In Romans v. 13, 14. sin is declared to have been in the world, from Adam to Moses, a period of twenty-five hundred years, and death is represented to have reigned, even over those who had not sinned after the similtude of Adams transgression. He reared his gloomy throne and reigned, in that remote antiquity amid the habitations of men, and strewed the earth with bones. His war was on the race, remorseless and exterminating; nor age, nor sex, escaped. Even the helplessness of unoffending infancy, was no protection ; and as they had not sinned actually, violated no law known to them ; and, as sin is not imputed where there is no law, why were they treated as sinners, and subjected to the dreadful penalty of death ? It was by imputation. It was by the offence of *one*. That offence was adjudged to be the offence of the race, and by it they were all, accounted guilty. Thus in entailed estates, the heirs at law, were all from generation to generation, disinherited by the rebellion of the original colonist against the crown. It was his act at the time when he committed the offence, which forfeited the estate to his unborn descendants, because he was their legal representative. By this one man's offence, many were made poor and they rebelled in him, and fell with him from the favor of the king, not by their own subsequent acts of rebellion, but by that of a distant progenitor. And in like manner "the covenant being made with Adam, as a public person, not for himself only, but also for his posterity, all mankind descending from him by ordinary generation, sinned in him, and fell with him, in his first transgression." Shorter Catechism, Question 16th. "In Adam all die;" (1 Corinthians xv. 22;) die by virtue of a federative, as well as by a natural relation, even also as Levi, long before he was born, paid tithes in Abraham, and compromised the integrity of his claim to supremacy in the priesthood, by an act of his illustrious ancestor five hundred years before Aaron was called and consecrated, "for he was yet in the loins of his father, Abraham, when Melchisedec met him." Hebrews vii. 10.

This doctrine of the imputation of Adam's sin, illustrates the parallel doctrine of the imputation of Christ's righteousness. "For as by one man's disobedience, many were made sinners, so by the obedience of one shall many be made righteous." Romans v. 19.

As Adam was a public person, so Christ was a public person. As Adam acted for others, so Christ acted for others. As Adam's disobedience was imputed to others, who had not been personally disobedient, so Christ's obedience, is imputed to those who have not personally obeyed. And as the offence of one, adjudged the "many" to death, so the obedience of one, adjudged the "many" to life. The truth, wisdom and equity of that court, from whence this judgment proceeds, cannot be questioned. "It is God that justifieth." Romans viii. 33. We believe then that "justification, is an act of God's free grace, wherein he pardoneth all our sins, and accepteth us as righteous in his sight, only, for the righteousness of Christ, imputed to us, and received by faith alone." See Shorter Catechism, Answer 33.

This doctrine of the Bible, and of our standards, has no place in the new divinity. Among its opponents, Mr. Barnes holds a conspicuous place, as a standard authority, and by his Notes, in permanent and portable manuals, widely endorsed and circulated among the New School, he is rapidly forming the opinions and characters of the rising generation.

He is far more guarded and prudent in expressing himself on this point than some who are reported to have said "imputed righteousness, is imputed nonsense." His high sense of propriety, and his strong desire to render his works acceptable to all, has led him to convey the same thought in less offensive terms. His own language on this subject is, "A few (expressions) that have given offence, have been changed, because without abandoning any principle of doctrine or interpretation, I could convey my ideas in language more acceptable, and less fitted to produce offence * * * with a desire to do all that can be done without abandoning principle, to promote peace and to silence the voice of alarm." (Notes on Romans, 9th edition, note to first preface.) This is amiable, but it does not prove that because the gentleman has changed his manner that he has therefore changed his sentiments, or that even he regards imputed righteousness as any other than imputed nonsense. A few quotations, will show that the latter impression is incorrect. "It is not that his righteousness became ours. This is not true, and there is no intelligible sense in which that can be understood."—Notes, Romans i. 17. Here the denial is less abrupt, less fitted to produce offence, than it might have been, but it is equivalent to the very worst form in which it has ever been made. Of our view, he says, "it is not true," and in the place of the word "nonsense" he uses the sentence "there is no intelligible sense in which that can be understood." That is (if bluntly said) there is no sense in that statement; it is nonsense. Again, " to sin by imputation is unintelligible and conveys no idea." Notes, Rom. xiii, 14. Here he does not say it is "nonsense" but that the statement conveys no idea, i. e. it is void of sense, it is nonsense. Those therefore who claim that he has changed or even modified his views, or that he differs from the very worst enemies of imputation, do him injustice. The difference is not in his views, but in his style and manner.

All the quotations which I make from Mr. Barnes, are from the latest editions of his notes, and in these his language is sufficiently strong and explicit, to be readily understood. In the following statement, he defines his position, with an exactness which defies misapprehension. "If he (Christ) was in any proper sense guilty then he deserved to die and his death could have no more merit than that of any other guilty being, and if he was properly guilty, it would make no difference in this respect whether it was by his own fault, or by imputation." All other passages relating to imputation, are explained by him, in perfect accordance with these views.— When it is affirmed that "what the law could not do, in that it was weak through the flesh, God sending his own Son in the likeness of sinful flesh, and for sin condemned sin in the flesh; that the righteousness of the law, might be fulfilled in us." Rom. viii. 3. We understand the apostle to say, that the fulfilling of the law in our nature by the Son of God is the fulfilling of the law in us; and that "there is therefore now no condemnation to them who are in Christ Jesus." That "he who will by no means clear the guilty," (Exodus, xxxiv. 7,) does not respect us as guilty. "He beholdeth no iniquity in Jacob, and no perverseness in Israel." Num. xxiii. 21. Yet Mr. Barnes, makes the fulfilling of the law's righteousness, to be our obedience to its precepts. The expression, "fulfilled in us," signifies according to him, "that we might be obedient, or comply with its demands."

The following statement is equally singular: "God sent forth his Son, made of a woman, made under the law, to redeem them that were under the law." "*Made under the law*," as one of the human race, partaking of human nature, he was subject to the law of God. As a man he was bound by its requirements, and subject to its control." Gal. iv. 3, 4. He however, who was sent forth was the Son of God, his son prior to his incarnation, and equally his son after that event. His human nature never was a person; never had a personal existence, separate from his divine. His two natures were from the first instance of susception, "indissolubly joined together in one person." As a man, then, simply considered, in his legal relations, and personal responsibilities, he never existed; but only as the Son, uniting the human and divine natures in one person forever. His subjection to the law, was voluntary, not necessary, not the inseparable condition of his humanity: he was not under the law, but was *made* under the law. Nor was he made under the law, because he was made of a woman, but to redeem them that were under the law." To the law he owed no obedience on his own account. It was made for creatures; they were necessarily bound by its requirements and subject to its control. But the Son was not a creature. He was the Creator of the ends of the earth. He was made under the law, to render an obedience, that he did not owe as a natural obligation: an obedience which the law (made for the finite) could not demand from the infinite; that he might restore that which he took not away, work out a righteousness; a righteousness, which was not an essential quality, but a public treasure, not essential to the son, respected simply as the son, but external to him, or mediatorial, and therefore, capable of imputation. Had he owed obedience to the law, as a man, his obedience would have been no more than the measure of his duty, as its natural subject, and imputation would have been an impossibility. But his obedience did not alter his moral character; he was in this respect, as righteous before that obedience was rendered by him, as afterward, "the same, yesterday, to day, and forever." Heb. xiii. 8. It was not required, by the necessities of his nature, but by the necessities of his people, and was wrought out purely for their benefit. If the Son had ceased to be God, when he became man, then his being made under the law, would have been the necessary condition of his incarnation; he would have been placed there, not by choice, but by a necessity of nature. But the Scriptures represent it to have been not an act of duty, but of voluntary humiliation.— "Being in the form of God he thought it not robbery to be equal with God; yet made himself of no reputation and took upon him the form of a servant, and was made in the likeness of men, and being found in fashion as a man, he humbled himself, and became obedient unto death, even the death of the cross." Phil. ii. 6, 8. Here, his whole obedience, active and passive, is included in the sum of his voluntary humiliation. If this obedience was demanded by a law of his nature, it was his duty to render it, and his rendering it could not be plead in evidence of his most wonderful condescension. What he owed and paid on his own account, proved him a dutiful subject, but not a condescending benefactor. The Son moreover could not have been bound by the law, respected as the son, otherwise he could not have been "made under it," for on this supposition, he was already under it. If then he remained divine, when he became human, his whole obedience was a gratuity,—a condescension,—a humiliation. The law had claims, claims which were infinite, claims which none could satisfy in the circumstances in which man was placed except God himself; but they were upon his ruined people, not naturally upon the Son, and he therefore took their place under the violated covenant, "to restore that which he took not away." Ps. lxix. 4. Moreover the obedience of death, was confessedly not that which he could owe on his own account; that obedience the law could not demand of the innocent, but only of the guilty, and as he had no sin in himself, he deserved not to die; this act of obedience the law could not require of him; in offering it, he was not subject to its control; he had perfect power over his own life; over it the law had no legitimate power but by his own consent; his obedience therefore, was not necessary but voluntary, an instance of infinite condescension, and strictly vicarious.

Those beasts whose daily sacrifice bathed the sides of

Mount Zion with the unceasing waste of life, were neither the transgressors of the law, nor its natural subjects. And in this as truly as in other respects, they were the shadows of the heavenly Lamb, who was neither a sinner, nor a natural subject. They were sacrificed by the law of a typical imputation; He by the law of a real one. Their innocence was no obedience; their death no satisfaction. "Wherefore, when he cometh into the world, he saith sacrifice and offering thou wouldest not, but a body hast thou prepared me. In burnt offerings and sacrifices for sin thou hast had no pleasure. Then said I, lo I come in the volume of thy book it is written of me to do thy will O God. (I come of my own free will, to offer that obedience, in the place of my people, which will take away every defect in them.) By the which will, we are sanctified, through the offering of the body of Jesus Christ, once for all." Heb. x. 5, 10.

Imputation, is not to me an unintelligible idea; not a metaphysical subtilty of the schools; not the ever erring philosophy of man concerning unrevealed mysteries, in providence and redemption. It is as intelligible to me, as the assumption of the debt of Onesimus by Paul; I have but to change the actors and the law; Christ assumes and pays the debt of love and obedience I owe to God and his law, and bears the penalty due to my offences. God accepts the substitute and sets his righteousness to my account. This is not unintelligible. It is plain to me, and plain to all, even to those most "unlettered in all that proceeds from halls and colleges." It is to me and is to every believer a fact, not "the mere philosophy of a fact; of a fact that cannot be explained and that admits of no explanation." The imputation of the sin of Adam, and of the righteousness of Christ, are facts as clearly revealed, as the offence of the one, and the obedience of the other. If it is revealed as a fact that Adam offended, so it is also that that offence belongs to the race in the judgment of God. " The judgment was by one unto condemnation."

Rom. v, 16. So also, if it is a revealed fact, that Christ obeyed the law at all, it is also, that that obedience, is made in the judgement of God, the obedience of his people. "He is made of God, unto us righteousness." 1 Cor. i. 30.

Be not deceived by the clamor, raised concerning the imputation of Adam's sin. The misrepresentations with which it is assailed, should not divert your attention from their effects upon another and a kindred question, viz: Upon the imputation of the righteousness of Christ. The eye that mocks at the one, mocks at the other. The hand that rends and scatters the first covenant, rends and scatters the second. While it affects but to overturn a gloomy dogma of the schools, it overturns both the altar, and the sacrifice of our High Priest, "for as by one man's disobedience many were made sinners, so by the obedience of one shall many be made righteous." Rom. v. 19. The principles are analogous, they stand or fall together. Hold fast then the "form of sound words," and consider the exceeding riches of that grace exhibited by them. They contain no doctrine of a stinted and impoverished Redeemer, who owed all for himself, and could give nothing, because he had nothing to give. "For it pleased the Father that in him should all fullness dwell." Col. i. 19. "The Lord is well pleased for his righteousness sake, he hath magnified the law and made it honorable."— Isaiah xlii. 21. "There is an abundance of grace, and an abundance of righteousness." Rom. v. 17. And if he has enough and to spare, why is it absurd to believe that it is imputed to his people; that out of his own ample sacerdotal robe is made that " clean white linen which is the righteousness of the saints?" Rev. xix. 8. The sum of his righteousness is greater than that of all creatures. If all had proved obedient, and for ever obedient, in heaven, earth, and hell, the whole, gathered together, and regarded in its mightiest aggregate, could never have equaled in value, and glory and fullness, that single righteousness wrought out by the

Son of God. The righteousness of creatures however great still has its degrees, but that of the eternal Son has no degrees it is and must be infinite. "His righteousness [is] as the waves of the sea." Isaiah xlviii. 18. All the navies of the world appear like specks upon the bosom of the sea. So the righteousnesses of all creatures, in all worlds, are but dark spots on the bosom of our Lord's righteousness. His righteousness, is vast, like the sea, a sea whose healing and refreshing waters, fill immensity and eternity. Let us therefore "count all things but loss, that we may win Christ, and be found in him, not having our own righteousness which is of the law, but that which is through the faith of Christ the righteousness which is of God by faith." Phil. iii. 8, 9.

Presbyterians, believe that "it is not the grace of faith, nor any act thereof, which is imputed to us for our justification;" (Larger Catechism Ans. 73,) " that justification is an act of Gods free grace, wherein he pardoneth all our sins, and accepteth us as righteous in his sight, only for the righteousness of Christ, imputed to us, and received by faith alone." (Short Catechism, Ans 33.) But Mr. Barnes, in opposition to this affirms that the act itself, is imputed to us for righteousness. On Romans iv. 3 : " It was counted unto him for righteousness," he remarks, " *It* here evidently refers to the act of believing. It does not refer to the righteousness of another, of God or of the Messiah. Faith is always an act of the mind, it is not a created essence which is placed within the soul. It is not a substance created independently of the soul and placed within it by Almighty power. It is not a principle. For the expression, a principle of faith, is as unmeaning as a principle of joy, or a principle of sorrow, or a principle of remorse. God promises, man believes, and this is the whole of it." * * * * " The word (impute) is never used to denote imputing in the sense of transferring, or of charging that on one which does not properly belong to him. The same is the case in the New Testament. The word occurs about forty times (See Schmidius' Concor.) and in a similar signification. No doctrine of transferring or of setting over to man what does not properly belong to him, be it sin or holiness, can be derived therefore from this word. Whatever is meant by it here, it evidently is declared that the act of believing is that which is intended both by Moses and by Paul." And again on the 21st verse, "It was imputed unto him for righteousness," he remarks: "He was tried and he had such confidence in God that he showed that he was supremely attached to him and would obey and serve him. This was reckoned as a full proof of friendship, and he was recognized and treated as righteous, i. e. as the friend of God." And on Romans i, 17, "For therein is the righteousness of God revealed from faith to faith," he remarks: "It does not say that it is on legal principles." Hence Mr. Barnes obviously teaches that faith is an act demonstrable of love to God, and to which God is graciously pleased to promise pardon, though it receives not, as indeed it cannot, the "righteousness of God or of the Messiah." Mr. Finney states that "Jesus Christ was bound to obey the law for himself and could no more perform works of supererogation or obey on our account than any body else." * * * "Abraham's faith was imputed to him for righteousness, because it was itself an act of righteousness, and because it worked by love and therefore produced holiness. Justifying faith is holiness, so far as it goes, and produces holiness of heart and life, and is imputed to the believer as holiness, not instead of holiness." (See Lectures to professing Christians, pp. 215, 216.) From this it will be seen at once that the opposition of many of the New School, to Mr. Finney, cannot be because he differs from them on this question. He may express himself with less caution, with less of circumlocution and tergiversation, and in a way more calculated to awaken "the voice of alarm," but on this point he certainly teaches substantially what they teach.

When opposing sects hold some principle which is common to them all, their modes of explanation and defence are usually similar. That the sufferings of Christ were in no sense penal, is a principle received in common by the New School and Unitarian divines; and hence their views of justification strikingly resemble each other. "Faith (says Dr. Dewey) is not some metaphysical and technical condition of salvation. It is simply a Christian grace. It is essentially a right heart. It is the old, the everlasting, the universal condition of happiness and of God's favor here and hereafter —a right heart. And this is prevailingly represented in the New Testament as putting itself forth in the act, in the form of faith. * * * * * It is opposed to a sense of merit founded on the moral law. * * * * It is the method of justification, or of acceptance with God. * * * * It works by love, but it is opposed to a proud claim of God's favor and of heaven set up on the ground of complete obedience. * * * * * He (Paul) takes them on their own favorite ground—justification: he takes up their very word: he shows them that they cannot be justified in the way they propose: he tells them that the only justification possible is of another kind—a gratuitous one, being treated as if just; and this through faith in the mercy of God." (See Dr. Dewey's Controversial discourses, pp. 322, 323, 326.) How striking the coincidence! Faith (says Mr. Barnes) is an act, demonstrable of love to God. It is a state of mind to which God is graciously pleased to promise pardon. It has no reference to the righteousness of another, of God, or of the Messiah. God promises—man believes; and this is the whole of it. It is (continues Mr. Finney) itself a righteousness. It is reckoned for just what it is. "It is (says Dr. Dewey) the old, the everlasting, the universal condition of happiness and God's favor here and hereafter—it is the *method* of justification or of acceptance with God." It is "God's *plan* of justifying men." Barnes' N. Rom. i. 17.

If, then, faith, respected simply as an act of the mind, is itself imputed to us for righteousness, then God has "denied himself;" (2 Tim. ii. 13;) truth falls by his own hand, and the reputation of his justice perishes forever. For, according to this, the sufferings of Christ were not just; they were not legal; they were not the penalty of sin; and hence impress us, not with the evil of sin, but with the evil of innocence, under the government of that God who cuts off the righteous in his righteousness, and reckons and treats the guilty as though they were innocent, when it is well understood, that the reckoning is thoroughly false, and the treatment, an abandonment of his law, and a violation of his word. If faith is at last the condition of salvation, without the righteousness, it would have been far more creditable, also, that it should have been the condition, without the sufferings of the Messiah; for these were not the penalty of our sins: they were not required by the justice of God. If they were, then they were penal: but, as they were not penal, justice did not require them; and there can be no assignable justification for this unearthly murder. It is a shame to speak of it as defensible on any ground, when it does not comprehend in it the curse of our sins. Take this away, this cause everywhere assigned in the Scriptures, as the cause of the sufferings of Christ, and his death is taken, at once, out from among all other instances of criminal violence, and made to stand out alone, as the greatest outrage ever perpetrated under any government. It was the unnecessary expenditure of unforfeited happiness; the criminal waste of the innocent blood. If, then, faith, as it is an act, is made the condition of salvation, *with* the sufferings of Christ, it would have served that purpose far better *without* them; for they serve only the more deeply to embarrass and disgrace the whole transaction. It is surely shame sufficient, to represent God as "denying himself," and abandoning his law, after all the pledges he had given, that he would not do it, without adding the additional infamy of death, inflicted by his own hand and providence, on the loveliest person in the universe ; "That be far from thee, to do after this manner, to slay the righteous with the wicked, and that the righteous should be as the wicked. That be far from thee. Shall not the Judge of all the earth do right?" Gen. xviii. 25. If justice is dishonored—if the law is cast out, this is all-sufficient, without adding more—without destroying every other remaining lineament of moral beauty in the character of the ever-blessed God.

We conclude, therefore, that the New School make void the law of God, and make void the death of Christ; for, if he did not bear our sins, as he had no sins of his own, he hung upon the tree to no good purpose, so far as we can discover; and it had been better that the sorrowful tragedy had never been enacted. So that this error involves in it several great enormities. It represents God as committing violence, both upon his justice and upon his Son,—as weak, and fickle, and false; in making a law which he could not maintain, in uttering curses which he is forced to reverse, and in reckoning men to be righteous, when there is no single respect in which that reckoning can be true.

But I have not done with this prolific error. It makes punishment unnecessary to the proper vindication of the law: punishment, according to it, is not required by the justice of God. Those who escape its penalty are reckoned righteous by a fiction. Justice has had no satisfaction, and requires none; for if it did, they would not have escaped without its being rendered. Justice, moreover, having required no satisfaction of the redeemed for their sins, does not necessarily require it of any; for that which would make satisfaction necessary for the sins of any, would make the same satisfaction necessary for the sins of all. Justice cannot dispense with a necessary quality; for that would be to destroy its very nature. But it has dispensed with the penalty of the law, and that without satisfaction, in the case of the redeemed; therefore, that penalty is not necessary to it: it is not required by the justice of God to be inflicted on any: and if inflicted at all, it is not demanded either by the law of God or by the justice of his nature. And, if neither law nor justice demand the infliction of the penalty, it will never be inflicted on any. "Shall not the Judge of all the earth do right?" So that, whichsoever way we turn, this error meets us with an aspect every way dishonorable to the character of God, and effectually and forever subverts his moral government.

How can we, then, regard the matters which divide us as in their own nature trifling; as questions in the mere philosophy of religion; as no sufficient justifiable cause for division and separation? Is it, then, of no account whether the righteousness of Christ or our own state of mind is imputed to us for a justifying righteousness? Is it of no moment to us, whether faith has reference to the righteousness of God or of the Messiah, or whether it has not? whether justice is treated as an attribute, and the law as an institution, or whether their claims are set aside by an act of divine sovereignty; and "the whole legal system suspended to make way for the operation of one of a different character?" (See Beman on Atonement, p. 133.) No; it cannot be. The principles involved in this controversy, are too sacred, and too momentous, ever to be relinquished, while faith, as a grain of mustard seed, lingers in the church, or a single throb of gratitude is felt among the redeemed. Who that loves God, would not rather that heaven and earth should pass away, than that one jot or tittle of the law should fail? Who could be pleased to see the eternal Son making common cause with rebels and conspirators against the law, and employing his infinite power and skill, in not satisfying, but in evading its claims; banishing it from the fire and darkness of Sinai—from the glory of heaven—from the face of the eternal throne, and sullying its fleecy robe of infinite purity, with the sins of men unrequited. Who that delights "in the law of God after the inward man," could be gratified with "such a spectacle of guilt and shame?"

I am aware that Mr. Barnes and the New School divines often express themselves in language inconsistent with these views of their sentiments. But when Mr. Barnes uses orthodox phrases, he takes occasion, with commendable frankness, ultimately to explain himself, as not intending thereby to contradict, or invalidate, or modify his opinions or sentiments, but as intending thereby to "*silence the voice of alarm.*" A similar course was pursued by Arius and Arminius. They softened their statements, and avowed their belief in an orthodox creed, "to silence the voice of alarm." Dr. Dewey, also, avows his belief in atonement, satisfaction, propitiation, depravity, regeneration, and justification. "It was (says he) a bitter and a bloody propitiation; it was a death endured for us. Ah! sinful being that I am, that such an one should suffer for me! It is I that deserved to suffer: but God hath made him a propitiation for my sins. Could nothing else set forth before me the curse of sin—no other hand bear the burden of my redemption?" Controversial Discourses, p. 99. The legitimate inquiry, then, is, not what statements the New School have made, or what forms of phraseology they sometimes use, which appear inconsistent with the errors charged upon them; but what is finally the real explanation, which they themselves furnish, of their own language.

Error is engraven on the face of truth. If it stood alone, in its own naked deformity, it would at once circulate the feeling of alarm. This is well understood by its advocates, and hence indirection is commonly resorted to, to gain proselytes. "By good words and fair speeches, they deceive the hearts of the simple." Rom. xvi. 18. Prof. Stewart is greatly annoyed at the course pursued by his former pupil, Dr. Dewey, in this respect. He finds fault with his saying one thing when he means another. "It merits [in his view] the scorn of every upright and honest man." See Dr. Dewey's Controversial Discourses, p. 54. Yet venerable men, who set the example, and lead the way, have the greater sin. If the advocates of the new divinity, in opposing the old, may consistently say one thing and explain themselves to mean another, then they should suffer Dr. Dewey to remain in the unmolested enjoyment of the same privilege, and to avail himself of all the advantages accruing to his cause from chicanery and indirection in controversy. But we have not so learned Christ. He is a God of integrity, and has not called us to walk in cunning craftiness, and to practice our arts on the unsuspecting. A system that requires such a method of defense, is not from him; and those who have resorted to it, will find it anything but a pleasing reminiscence upon a dying bed.

All that, then, which is said of the righteousness of God revealed, in the gospel Rom. i. 19; of Christ as the Lord our righteousness, Jer. xxiii. 6; of the believer's resolution to make mention of his righteousness and of his only, Ps. lxxi. 16.; of Christ's being made of God unto us, righteousness, 1 Cor. i. 30; of winning Christ and being found in him, not having our own righteousness, Phil. iii. 9; all that clear and abundant testimony contained in the gospel, that the righteousness of Christ is made ours in the judgment of God and received by faith alone, is made to signify, a mere act of our own minds. "This is the whole of it." "As this is not a matter of law, as the law could not be said to demand it, as it is on a different principle, and as the acceptance of faith or of a believer cannot be a matter of merit or claim, so justification is of grace or mere favor." See Mr. Barne's Notes, Rom. iv. 3. Again, (Rom. iv.) in the same place: "As the law did not demand this, and as faith was something different from the demand of the law, so if a man were justified by that, it was on a principle altogether different from justification by works; it was not by personal merit; it was not by complying with the law." Faith, then, as it is a mere act of the mind, regarded alone and by itself, separate from obedience to the law, and from the reception of the "righteousness of God, or of the Messiah," is reckoned to us for a righteousness; reckoned for precisely what it is not, and what it cannot be, according to the reasonings of this enemy of imputation. "God (says he) reckons things as they are, and not falsely, and his imputations are all according to truth." See Notes, Rom. v. 19.. But in this instance the reckoning is false; the thing is reckoned as it is not, and the imputation is not according to truth. It is wholly arbitrary, false, and without the least foundation in truth, in law, or in justice. And yet, we are assured, that "God does not esteem men to be different from what they are." See Notes, Rom. i. 17. God reckons things as they are, and not falsely, and his imputations are all according to truth :" i. e.: the believer is reckoned to be just by a "plan," by a "method," by an arbitrary determination, when he is not so in fact. "It was not by personal merit; it was not by complying with the law;" not by the "righteousness of another." Indeed, the whole reckoning is both false and farcical. In the language of Dr. Beman, "the whole legal system is suspended." Justice is abandoned; the law is given up; and truth and righteousness, in the salvation of believers, are doomed to have no further share in the moral government of God; of that God whose "imputations are all according to truth." Oh! how fraught with self-contradiction and pitiable imbecility, is this whole starvling imitation of the gospel. It is a city broken down and without walls; a kingdom full of darkness. On it, no radiance falls from the sun of righteousness; across its fearful solitudes, no godly man can find his weary way. "It is a land of droughts, and pits, and snares, and of the shadow of death."

The gospel itself is full of sweetness: "With honey out of the rock have I satisfied thee." It presents to us no mere act of arbitrary pardon. The atonement of Christ is a finished work: it makes ample provision for the believer; and the definition given of it by the law-giver himself, shows that it was composed of several parts, all of which went to make up a complex act, called the Atonement. The high priest, in the confession of the sins of the whole congregation, laid them on the head of the scape-goat, and he was lead away into a land uninhabited; commonly thrown from a precipice, that he might never return. This is the imputation of atonement. "The Lord did lay upon him the iniquity of us all. Isa. liii. 6. The other goat was killed and sacrificed on the altar. This was the sacrifice of atonement, and represents the "offering of the body of Christ once for all;" (Heb. x. 10;) and the fires of justice, which kindled upon the sacrifice, mounted up in the lifting up of smoke, and filled the heavens with the frown of God, representing that dreadful frown which fell upon the forsaken Son, on the accursed tree; which wasted his soul and consumed his life, and which filled heaven and earth with terrific darkness. The blood, taken and sprinkled seven times before the throne, in the innermost sanctuary, was the intercession of atonement, and represented our High Priest in the heavens, before the throne of God on high. "For Christ is not entered into the holy places made with hands, which are the figures of the true; but into heaven itself, now to appear in the presence of God for us;" (Heb. ix. 24;) and that "with his own blood;" (Heb. ix. 12;) "ever living to make intercession for us." Heb. vii. 25. The subsequent sprinkling of "all the people and all the vessels of the ministry, (Heb. ix. 19, 20, 21,) was the reconciliation of atonement, and represents "God, in Christ, reconciling the world unto himself, not imputing their trespasses unto them." 2 Cor. v. 19. Not any one of the several parts of this complex transaction, is the atonement, but all of them put together were necessary to fulfill the meaning of the word, as used by the law-giver.

We turn, then, to Christ, as the world did to Joseph from the reign of a universal famine, not only for some one of the means of subsistence, but for all of them. They are to be found, absolutely, none of them, any where else. If we need righteousness, we come to him; faith—"it is the gift of God; (Eph. ii. 8;) repentance and pardon—"he is exalted * * to give repentance unto Israel, and the forgiveness of sins;" (Acts v. 31 ;) indeed, "it pleased the Father that in him should all fullness dwell, and out of his fullness have all we received, and grace for grace." John i. 16. "Jesus has received of the Father the promise of the spirit." Acts ii. 33. "He giveth not the spirit by measure unto him." John iii. 34. Every grace, therefore, which invests the moral nature of his disciples, whatsoever things in their characters is lovely and of good report, if there be any virtue, any thing worthy of praise, it is wrought in them by his spirit, and according to the ample provisions of the atonement. We turn, then, from the cold systems of philosophers, to the more genial ones of the Prophets and Apostles of the Lamb; from a world of chaos, to a world of harmony and beauty—to the living melodies of Zion, to its gorgeous heavens, its sun of righteousness, its softened landscapes, and its milder skies; where youth is given to age, and feet to the lame, and where decline and death cannot abide. God in Christ can do that which is far more desirable than to pronounce us just, falsely, than to save by an arbitrary acquittal of the guilty; can do better than thus to break the pillars of his own throne, and cover its eternal glories with sackcloth. He can do more, by the atonement, than to acquit or pardon : "He can have compassion on the ignorant, and on them that are out of the way." Heb. v. 1, 2. "*Dunamenos*," literally, *He is able*. The ability is acquired by the atonement. The compassion existed in his own bosom, but it could have no egress. It was a pent-up ocean of pity, that sought a channel for its refreshing streams, that they might moisten the rock and renovate the desert. Christ opened that channel for the Father's pity, and his own. And ("*Metriopathein*," Heb. v. 2,) he has the ability in the sufficient *measure*, or without limit. It had limits in Moses; he could not carry the people across the wilderness, in a bosom that could always put a perfect restraint upon its just resentments. "Have I conceived all this people? have I begotten them, that thou shouldst say unto me, Carry them in thy bosom, as a nursing father beareth the sucking child, unto the land which thou swearest unto thy fathers? Whence should I have flesh to give unto all this people? for they weep unto me, saying, Give us flesh, that we may eat. I am not able to bear all this people alone, because it is too heavy for me. And if thou deal thus with me, kill me, I pray thee, out of hand, if I have found favor in thy sight; and let me not see my wretchedness." Num. xi. 12, 13, 14, 15. But Christ does "not fail;" he is never "discouraged;" (Isa. xlii. 4;) his capacity to bear with his people is always full and sufficient. The long-suffering of our Lord is salvation, (2 Pet. iii. 15,) because it never gives way to provocation. If it were the patience of a mere creature, it would: but it is the patience of the *Son*. He "will in *no wise* cast out" (John vi. 37.) those that come, those that sin not against the remedy itself, by their unbelief. The natural mother's place can never be supplied by a stepmother. However great her conscientiousness and efforts, nothing can supply the absent principle of maternal love. Solomon, by appealing to this principle, distinguished the true mother from the false. Christ is not defective in this respect: the tie of consanguinity is established; for, forasmuch as the children were partakers of flesh and blood, he likewise took part of the same. Heb. ii. 14. Not human nature, under imputed guilt, as a lineal descendant of the first Adam ; it was not by ordinary generation. It was the nature created by the Holy Ghost,—not with its moral infirmities ; for moral infirmities would be impossible to God the Son; but human nature, in its otherwise fallen state,— "compassed with infirmity." With a delicate frame, our Lord sat down in weariness and hunger, at the side of Jacob's well, while his more robust disciples could go on their way. He was susceptible of friendship, and loved the amiable John. He was susceptible of painful impressions, from the unkindness and cruelty, the falsehood and treachery of those who could practise on his confidence and abuse the privilege of intimacy. His look, that broke the heart of Peter, was that of injured love : and his complaint in David, when he was betrayed by a false-hearted dependant, shows how deeply his pure and holy soul was stung by that act of baseness. "For it was not an enemy that reproached me ; then I could have borne it : neither was it he that hated me that did magnify himself against me ; then would I have hid myself from him : but it was thou, a man, mine equal, my guide, and mine acquaintance. We took sweet counsel together, and walked unto the house of God in company." Ps. lv. 12, 13, 14. "Yea, mine own familiar friend, in whom I trusted, which did eat of my bread, hath lifted up his heel against me." Ps. xli. 9. To be forty days without food, amid the solitudes of a desert, to be tempted by the devil, to be the houseless child of want, to be despised for his poverty and rejected in his testimony, to be proved at length, a malefactor by false witnesses, and to be hung in ignominy on a tree. These were some of the evils which he endured, and which show him "able to be touched with a feeling of our infirmities." Heb. iv. 15. "Can a mother forget her sucking child? Yea, she may forget, [it is possible, some have done it,] yet will not I forget thee. I have graven thee on the palms of my hands." Isa. xlix. 15, 16. They were nailed to the cross for thy sins. I have answered thy prayer: "Set me a seal upon thy heart." Sol.'s Song, viii. 6. It was done with the soldier's spear, when its murderous point reached the fountains of salvation. And can I forget? No, never! But "*Metriopathein*" not only measures his ability to bear patiently, but to relieve, actively and effectively, and in the greatest extremities of unworthiness and peril. While the verb is in the passive voice, it has an active signification. He sent his gospel first to Jerusalem to be preached to his murderers. As they were in the greatest danger, so they needed his pity most. He laid hold on Saul of Tarsus, between Damascus and Jerusalem. He snatched the dying thief from the very gates of hell. Nothing could stand between him and the objects of his love: the everlasting mountains would in an instant be scattered. "All that the Father hath given to me, *shall* come to me." John vi. 37. Is repentance necessary to David? He sent repentance to him, and David brought before him the "sacrifice of a broken and a contrite heart." Does Peter need it? He sent it to him, and "he went out and wept bitterly." "He is the surety of the covenant;" (Heb. vii. 22;) he seals it with his blood, fulfills all its conditions, and by his providence, and spirit, and agency, carries out all its merciful provisions. He loses not one among all that the Father gave him. "Behold I, and the children that God hath given me." Heb. ii. 13. Not one is missing, even among those most feeble or most exposed amid the dangers of the way. "The bruised reed he did not break; the smoking flax he did not quench." It was a great and a difficult task, and it needed to be in the hands of one who could bear and pity, and relieve, in an infinite measure. His atonement, then, is composed of several parts, all of which perfectly correspond with each other, and secure and cover the same interests. Those whose sins are borne away in the imputation of atonement are included in its sacrifice, its intercession, and its reconciliation.

The blood of Christ was not a mere appeal, to make a great impression. It was "the blood of a covenant;" (Heb. xiii. 20;) a covenant established upon "better promises" than one that could be broken. It secured the reconciliation: "It put his laws in the heart; it wrote them on the mind; and it conveyed an infallible mercy even to the unrighteousness of his people." Heb. viii. 10, 12. It provided an High Priest who "could have compassion on the ignorant and on them that were out of the way," with a patience that could never be provoked, and with a pity that could never grow weary of its troublesome charge. Where a mother's love would fail—all human kindness fail; where both men and angels would be discouraged; in every possible extremity of weakness, perverseness and guilt among his ever erring disciples, he is equal to his work, and will as assuredly accomplish the reconciliation, as he has already the sacrifice of atonement. He did not make salvation merely possible, but certain. He does not merely open the way, but also the heart. There is not only virtue in him for the helpless, but it goes out of him, and their feet and ankle bones receive strength. His atonement not only provides a possible pardon, but an active and an efficient remedy. It is an ever welling tide, "the streams whereof make glad the city of God." It removes not only one obstacle, but every obstacle. It is as broad and beautiful, and sufficient in every part of it, as it is in any part of it. Nothing shall be wanting to complete its glory, and to awaken the halleluiahs of ransomed millions. "Unto Him that loved us, and that washed us from our sins in his own blood, and hath made us kings and priests unto God and his Father, unto him be glory and dominion forever and ever, Amen."

Faith can never turn away its eye from the perfect work of Christ, to admire a mere act of arbitrary indemnity, that falsifies every principle of truth, that suspends every tittle of the law, and excludes every element of justice. It is not

Christ. It hath not flesh and bones as we see him have. It is a fearful apparition, calculated to awaken horror, rather than confidence. The conjurations of philosophy, not the inspirations of heaven. It is at war with heaven, with its "mercy and truth," with its "righteousness and peace." It is at war with Zion; it takes away the sheaf from the hungry, and causes her naked to lodge without clothing. To lean upon it, is to lean upon a shadow that declineth, and to die in its embrace, is to perish from the way.

> "Rock of ages, cleft for me,
> Let me hide myself in thee:
> Let the water and the blood,
> From thy wounded side which flowed,
> Be of sin the double cure;
> Cleanse me from its guilt and power."

CHAPTER IV.

DOCTRINAL DIFFERENCES CONTINUED.

The Atonement—Its sufficiency—The New School limit it in its nature—The differences respect its nature, not its extent.

It is usual for opposing parties to misunderstand, and to misrepresent each other. Knowledge is limited, language an imperfect medium of communicating our ideas, and hence we are often called upon, to explain and vindicate our exact opinions. When an error has been successfully impaled, its advocates sometimes also lose their temper and assail our characters. We are not however in such an event, required to abandon the point at issue, to go out in our personal vindication. The public will do us ample justice in the end, and also the cause which we oppose, and which demands from its advocates so malicious a defence.

In matters moreover of a private and personal nature, few, will feel interested, while those which relate to our peculiar religious opinions, are of general interest, affecting the hopes and fears, the wants and woes which are common to all men. These, it can seldom be inappropriate in the spirit of charity to explain, discuss, and vindicate, and it often becomes a duty to do it. " Let not your good be evil spoken of."

It has occurred to me that in closing these chapters respecting the work of Christ, something ought to be said on those points, in the atonement, in which our views as Presbyterians are misrepresented, especially as in them, misrepresentation, addresses itself to the popular prejudice, which it awakens, to the iujury of the cause of truth and righteousness.

We are said to believe that the atonement is limited in its nature : it being sufficient for the salvation of the elect, but if any more should believe or be included it would require additional sufferings on the part of Christ to save them. "Those in general who hold the theological system which is called generically Calvinistic, and who hold it perhaps with equal decision and sincerity in common, though palpably not with equal correctness in degree are divided here, some holding the fullness of the atonement for all men. others the limitation of its nature, as atonement to all the finally saved." * * * "We therefore contend for the fullness of the atonement." (Introduction to Beman on the Atonement by Dr. Cox, p. 16.) "The whole question respecting limited or general atonement is settled by the notions which we entertain of its intrinsic nature. If the atonement consisted in Christ's suffering the amount of misery due to all those who will be saved ; if it were a transaction regulated by the principles of commutative justice, then we might with propriety talk of its being limited to the elect. In this case, the sufferings of the mediator, must have been measured according to the number of individuals who were to be saved.— (Beman on Atonement p. 142.)

Such representations are common and the impression created is injurious because it is false.* We do not believe that the atonement is limited in its nature. Its limitation in this respect is impossible and absurd. It has a limit. All men are not included in it or saved by it ; but this limit is in the purpose of God, not in the nature of the atonement ; that would remain the same, whether the number of the saved, should

―――

* Though the New School are fond of representing us as limiting the Atonement in its nature, yet I am acquainted with no author who maintains this view of the subject, but Ezra Stiles Ely, D. D. a member of the New School General Assembly.

be more or less. The same is true of the mercy of God—it is infinite, because it is divine. It cannot be limited in its nature, but still it has a limit beyond which it does not extend; fallen angels and lost spirits are not included in it or saved by it: the limit, however, is not in the intrinsic nature of the divine mercy but in the determinations of the divine will.

The "worth and efficacy" of the atonement arises out of the divinity of Christ, its adaptation from his humanity, and its limitation from the terms of the covenant which it seals. "It was requisite that the Mediator should be God, that he might sustain and keep the human nature from sinking under the infinite wrath of God and the power of death, give *worth* and *efficacy* to his sufferings, obedience and intercession, and to satisfy God's justice, procure his favor, purchase a peculiar people, give his spirit to them, conquer all their enemies, and bring them to everlasting salvation." "It was requisite that the mediator should be man, that he might advance our nature, perform obedience to the law, suffer and make intercession for us in our nature, have a fellow feeling of our infirmities, that we might receive the adoption of sons, and have comfort and access, with boldness unto the throne of grace." (Larger Catechism, Ans. 38, 39.)

Christ is God. This gives "worth and efficacy" to his atonement; its worth and efficacy are measured by his divinity; no circumference can be found to it. Like the horizon which we approach, it widens, and widens, and widens, forever. Like the extreme points which terminate the distances of the east and the west; their separation is immeasurable; ages which never begin and never end roll between. An ocean which rests upon no bottom, is bounded by no shore. Such is the atonement in its fullness. We are conversant with no objects within the whole range of immensity and eternity, excepting those which are absolutely infinite, which can give us any adequate illustrations of its glorious sufficiency.

"Forasmuch also as the children were partakers of flesh

and blood, he likewise took part of the same," obeyed and suffered, arose and ascended in our common nature; and hence arises the adaptation of his atonement to all human sinners. His human nature bears a common relation to all who possess humanity Hence the atonement in its sufficiency and in its adaptation would require no alteration were any imaginable number included in it.

This view of the subject is not a novelty among Presbyterians, an alternative to which we have been recently driven in sheer self-defence. This will be seen by recurring to the above quotation from the catechism in which the sufficiency of the satisfaction of Jesus Christ, is referred to his Deity. Calvin also held " that Christ suffered sufficiently for all men, but efficiently for the elect alone."

" To the honor then of Jesus Christ our Mediator, God and man, our all sufficient Redeemer, we affirm, that such and so great was the dignity and worth of his death and blood shedding, of so precious a value, of such an infinite fullness and sufficiency was this oblation of himself, that it was every way able and perfectly sufficient to redeem, justify, reconcile and save, all the sinners in the world, and to satisfy the justice of God for all the sins of all mankind, and to bring them every one to everlasting glory. Now, this fullness and sufficiency of the merit of the death of Christ, is a foundation unto two things, viz :

The general publishing of the gospel unto all nations, with the right that it hath to be preached to every creature, (Mat. xx. 6. Mark xvi. 15.) Because the way of salvation which it declares, is wide enough for all to walk in ; there is enough in the remedy it brings to light, to heal all their diseases, to deliver them from all their evils : if there were a thousand worlds, the gospel of Christ might, upon this ground, be preached to them all; there being enough in it for the salvation of them all, if so be, they will desire virtue from him by touching him in faith, the only way to draw refreshment from this fountain of salvation. That the preachers of the gospel in their particular congregations, being utterly unacquainted with the purpose and secret counsel of God, being also forbidden to pry or search into it, (Deut. xxix. 29,) may from hence, justifiably call upon every man to believe, with assurance of salvation unto every one, in particular upon his so doing." (Owen's Death of Death, p. 204.)

"The ground on which the universality of the gospel offer proceeds, is the *all-sufficiency* of Christ's atonement. This the universal gospel message supposes and affirms. It is not said in the gospel, that Christ died with the intention that all should be saved, but his atonement is a sufficient ground of salvation to all, and that all who rest on this ground by faith shall be saved. This is all that the gospel asserts; and there is nothing here but what is true, and fit to be made known to all. Nor is any thing more requisite to vindicate the universality of the gospel offer from the charge of inconsistency or insincerity. The atonement of Christ being sufficient for all, possessing a glorious, infinite, all-sufficiency, it is with propriety made known and offered to the acceptance of all. There is, in this case, no natural impossibility in the salvation of any man. The secret design of God, by which the application is restricted, has no causal influence in producing unbelief. The obstacles to salvation are all moral, that is to say, are such only as arise from the native rebellion and hardness of man's own heart. A sufficient ground of salvation exists; the appropriate means of salvation are provided; and of course, a proper foundation is laid for man's accountability, so that, in rejecting salvation by Christ, he is absolutely without excuse. 'He that believeth not shall be condemned.'" (Symington on the Atonement, pp. 199, 200.)

Thus from the days of Calvin, to the present day the same view is taken of the sufficiency of the atonement. Dr. Junkin, who has been represented in this region, as one of our most ultra men, holds the following language on this point:

"I must also think, that the sufferings of Jesus have nothing to do with the number of the finally saved. The penalty of the law is the same, whether one or two, or a thousand persons are concerned. Whether the Father gives ten millions to his Son as the reward of his service—or ten million times ten millions, the obedience and sufferings of Jesus are the same. It was for him to meet the claims of law. But the demand of law was *obedience* and *death*. This obedience to the precept, and this meeting of the penalty is the same, whether one man or the whole race are to be saved. I have, therefore, no sympathy with the doctrine, that the sufferings of Jesus must have been *graduated* according to the number of the saved : so that if the number were increased, there must be a *pro rata* increase to his sufferings." (Junkin on Justification, pp. 242, 243.) But it is quite unnecessary to pursue these quotations farther. I have adverted to this kind of testimony simply for the purpose of indicating sufficiently our precise position on this question.

While, moreover, we believe in the fullness of the atonement; we also believe that it is definite: that its blood is the blood of a covenant, and hence is called "the blood of the everlasting covenant;" that apart from that covenant which it ratified and sealed the death of Christ would be without significance or efficacy. It would be no atonement. The covenant which the blood sealed is a part of the atonement, entering into the very nature of the transaction. The one is essential to the very existence of the other, because they are the componant parts of a complex action. If they are separated both are destroyed. Christ suffered in view of the promises which secured to him definitely "the travail of his soul," and "this He shall fully and infallibly realize and be satisfied." The covenant comprehends all that his death purchased—his death comprehends all that the covenant promised. The one exactly measures and defines the other.

Great errors often arise from small causes and a wrong definition of the word atonement, may be one of the proximate causes of the prevalent errors on this subject. When a term is used, and carefully defined by God himself, it is always safest and most reverent, to adhere to that definition in the use of it. If we will recur to the definition given to the word atonement on the day of the great annual atonement, we will at once discover that it consisted not in one, but in may things, that it was not a single, but a complex action. The laying of the sins of the whole congregation on the head of the scape-goat was not the atonement, but the imputation of the atonement. The sacrifice of the other goat was not the atonement, but its sacrifice. The sprinkling of the blood seven times was not the atonement, but its intercession. The subsequent sprinkling of all the people, and of the place, and of all the vessels of the ministry, was not the atonement, but its reconciliation ; not any one of these symbolic actions constituted the atonement, but all of them together. When atonement was made, it was not completed until all its several parts were completed. It was a complex action, all the several parts of which were fulfilled by Jesus Christ, who was not many; but one; uniting in himself the scape-goat, and the goat for sacrifice, the altar, and the Priest.

But the New School while they profess to believe in the fulness of the atonement, in its universality, that Christ tasted death for every man, practice a deception upon themselves and others, by the terms which they employ and do not really believe that Christ died for any man. Indeed, they speak in the most depreciating style of his death, and finally resolve it into a mere indemnity against future rebellion. "Commutative justice was not satisfied by the atonement. * * * Distributive justice was not satisfied by the transaction. * * * The penalty of the law strictly speaking, was not inflicted *at all.* * * * *All* that the atonement has effected for the sinner is to place him within the reach of pardon. * * * It *merely* prepared the way for the proclamation of mercy, to rebels and the extension of actual pardon to every believer in Christ Jesus. * * * But if the atonement *merely* rendered pardon compatible with the glory of God and the public good, if it did not require but *merely* permitted God to extend forgiveness to sinners. * * * If the atonement consists not in cancelling the demand for *any man or for all men*, but in opening the door of hope in rendering the pardon of sinners consistent with the character, law and universe of God, then the question of extent is settled at once. * * * The atonement does not of itself save a single soul. It *barely* opens the door for the accomplishment of this object by the free and sovereign grace of God." (Beman on Atonement pp. 132, 133, 134, 135, 136, 137, 141, 142, 155.)

Here, in these few short quotations, there are at least seven instances in which the language of depreciation is used respecting the atonement; and one instance in which it is said that "in itself it does not save a *single soul*," and in another, that it does not cancel the demand even *"for one man,"* and in any event it *merely* does this and it *barely* effects that; so that the New School while they contend for the extent of the atonement and profess to believe that Christ died for every man, limit it to a mere nothing, and deny in the progress of the controversy that he died for any man.

Mr. Barnes also makes the atonement a very insignificant matter. According to him the text in Rom. i. 17, does not say that justification was on legal principles, and he labors hard every where to show that we are not justified in this way, because Christ did not obey for us, nor suffer penalty for us, that our sins were not imputed to him, nor is his righteousness imputed to us, but we are justified by a *plan* in which *faith* as it is an act of the mind and as it does not receive, and as indeed it cannot either the righteousness of God or of the Messiah, is reckoned to us for righteousness. All that the death of Christ effects, is to make this course consistent and safe.

In his preface to Butler's Analogy, he vindicates what he terms "the main principle of atonement," in the following manner : " The toil of a father is the price by which a son is saved from ignorance, depravity, want, or death; the tears of a mother, and her long watchfulness save from the perils of infancy and an early death. Friend aids friend by toil. A parent foregoes rest for a child, and the patriot pours out his blood on the altars of freedom, that others may enjoy the blessings of liberty, that is, that others may not be doomed to slavery, want, and death."

But the instances here named, do not vindicate any principle of the atonement, i. e. they do not distinguish it from paternal love, humanity, friendship, patriotism, martyrdom, and, therefore, the analogies are no analogies ; they do not reach, strictly speaking, any principle peculiar to the atonement ; they exhibit the toils and trials of paternal love, friendship, patriotism, and this is all. In the atonement the innocent suffers for the guilty on legal principles. Christ takes the sinner's place under the broken law of offended heaven, and bears its bitter curse and puts away sin, by the sacrifice of himself; and as he redeems us from the curse of the law, so he suffers upon legal principles and any other sufferings of parents, patriots, and martyrs, are not of the nature of atonement; i. e. they are not sufferings inflicted by the lawgiver on the innocent for the sins of the guilty, and in accordance with the principles of justice.

The principle of atonement vindicated by Mr. Barnes, is strictly Unitarian. " He certainly is mistaken when he says that Unitarians deny all such substitution. We deny the Calvinistic explanation of atonement or substitution. We might reject the author's hypothesis, too, if we knew what it was. But does it follow that we deny all substitution—on the contrary we especially hold to such substitution." (Dewey's Controversial Discourses pp. 13, 14, Note.) And he is certainly mistaken likewise, if he thinks to pass off on enlightened Presbyterians the self-denial of parents, friends and patriots for the main principle of atonement—to restrict the atonement in its main principle to a point so insignificant not only limits but destroys it altogether.

Thus, then, the New School limit the atonement with respect to the obedience of Christ, it was for himself; with respect to the death of Christ, it does not save a single soul; it does not meet the penalty of the law; it barely opens the door to a possible pardon; it is not on legal principles; its main principle is self-denial; it is indeed, in every respect limited and in almost every possible way made contemptible. The true defenders, therefore, of an atonement limited in its very nature, are to be sought for among the New School themselves. They limit it effectually, because they take from it every ingredient that could make it either sufficient or efficacious. According to them, the death of Christ is sufficient and efficacious in one respect and in one only; it renders pardon consistent, permits its exercise, places it within reach, and this is all.

But the death of Christ comprehends in it the entire redemption of his church. It is the vast foundation on which it rests, the living source of its origin, progress and triumph. We are chosen in him before the foundation of the world, and he finished the work given him to do, removing every obstacle out of the way of the salvation of his people, and procuring for them eternal life; "for by one offering he hath perfected forever, them that are sanctified." Heb. x. 14.—All is now secured to him, all is now a joyful waiting for the redemption of the purchased possession. It has been already conveyed by promise, and secured by price. It remains only to be redeemed by power.

His obedience unto death makes him the Lord our righteousness and delivers us from the curse of the law. His mediatorial throne and triumphs rest upon his mediatorial humiliation. Phil. ii. 9. The "purpose and grace" of effectual calling are "given us in Christ Jesus." " The washing of regeneration and renewing of the Holy Ghost, are shed upon us abundantly through Jesus Christ our Lord." "For our sakes he sanctified himself," with "the blood of the covenant" and offered himself without spot to God. The Father also acted in a manner becoming himself as the first cause and final end of all things, "in bringing many sons unto glory, by making the captain of their salvation perfect through suffering." "It pleased the Father that in him should all fullness dwell." And thus his death instead of effecting barely one thing, effects every thing. The New Testament is given us in his blood. The sabbath commemorates his triumph over death, The supper shows forth his death. The strength of the law is broken, the sting of death destroyed and the victory given us over every enemy and finally over the last, " through our Lord Jesus Christ." 1. Cor. xv. 57. Christ is not in one way effective only, but in every way, "Christ is all, and in all." When the passage is read " he was led as a lamb to the slaughter," and the inquiry is made, of whom speaketh the prophet this, of himself or of some other man? we "begin at the same scripture and preach Jesus;" we hold him up to the understanding as the object of faith, and the spirit begets him in the heart the hope of glory. The sun shines to light his ransomed people on their way. The rain falls and the earth yields her increase for their refreshment. "The heathen are his inheritance and the uttermost parts of the earth are his possession; when they obstruct the progress of his kingdom and it suits his will, he breaks them with a rod of iron; the strongest governments are dashed as a potter's vessel." Ps. ii. He shall come at length in his kingdom purchased by him on the cross, sit upon the throne of his glory, raise the dead, and judge the universe. To this throne and glory he was raised, because "he humbled himself and became obedient unto death even the death of the cross." This was the price agreed upon in the covenant. It was not to be silver or gold, these though the most durable and valuable of metals, are comparatively corruptible things. It was "the precious blood of Christ." This lifted the incumbrance from the forfeited inheritance; overthrew the house of bondage, broke the strength of the law and the head of the dragon, and went forth in much assurance and in the Holy Ghost and in power, to subdue the people under him, lifted him up above the stars and made him as mediator, Lord over thrones, and dominions, and principalities, and powers. In a word, the death of Christ is the comprehensive and sole efficiency in the work of redemption.

Thus, it is clearly an error, and one of no ordinary dimensions to limit the atonement to the bare possibility and the consistent exercise of pardon. "Christ is made of God unto us wisdom and righteousness and sanctification and redemption." "He is the *author* and *finisher* of faith." His atonement procured the dispensation of the spirit and purchases and conveys every blessing to the redeemed. It comprehends their calling and perseverance, their faith and righteousness, their resurrection and glory.

As it is the source of all good to the redeemed from the original purpose in the Lamb slain from before the foundation of the world, down to the last drop of dew that falls to cool the fevered lip of the weary pilgrim in his way, and upward to every ray which he sheds among the stars forever and ever: So it also comprehends every one among all the redeemed. It goes backward to the fall and onward to the end of the world. It opens its fountain in the house of David, for sin and uncleanness, but that sweet river which makes glad the city of God, cannot be confined to Judea alone.—— It breaks over that narrow boundary and flows onward, widening and widening until it reaches the utmost bounds of the everlasting hills. "Rejoice, thou barren that barest not, break forth and cry thou that travailest not, for the desolate hath many more children than she that hath an husband." It was the cross that broke down the middle wall of partition between Jew and Gentile, and slew the enmity. But the barriers of earth and time are too narrow for its ultimate range and mighty development. It breaks over them and pours an ocean of blessedness around the Father's throne, and upon the bosom of eternity. And as it is the living centre and source of all good to the redeemed, so its memorials meet us every where. When we leave this world and enter upon the heavenly state, by faith, we are permitted, even here, to gaze upon those memorials amid the abundant revelations which present them. There in the midst of the throne, in the central point of dignity and glory, visible every where, the grand object of wonder, love and praise is a lamb as it had been slain, wearing the memorials of his sacrifice and carrying every recollection back to the price of redemption. The melodies which are always sweetest and which forever return upon the delighted ear, are gathered from the garden and the cross. "Worthy is the Lamb, for he was slain, and hath redeemed us to God by his blood." A mighty host are seen advancing over the plains of Paradise, with crowns on their heads and palms in their hands; and in in answer to the inquiry, "Who are these arrayed in white robes, and whence come they?" responsive choirs reply, "These are they who have come up out of deep tribulation, and have washed their robes and made them white in the blood of the Lamb." There is there a pure river of the water of life, clear as crystal, flowing and sparkling from the eternal throne. We go back upon its source and trace it downward to this world and backward along the track of centuries till we reach again the garden and the cross; here were opened its healing fountains and from hence they flow and cheer and refresh forever. Between the terrace walk and that river on a plat of perrenial verdure stands there the tree of life. The flaming sword of the cherubim who guarded it, that waved forever there, and warned us back from its blessed vicinity, was quenched in the blood of the Lamb. It awoke against the shepherd and the man that was the fellow of the Father's throne. It awoke to consume its fire and to smite for the last time: henceforth that tree is forever accessible to the redeemed: its leaves are for the healing of the nations. There, too, all tears are wiped from all faces: the soft hand extended in that act of availing pity, wears a scar; it was nailed to the cross for our sins.

And as its memorials meet us every where, so the inheritance purchased by it, shall last forever. The kingdom of providence extending over the angels who never sinned, is not mediatorial, and, therefore, sheds and perpetuates its blessings directly upon the innocent; but the mediatorial kingdom rests upon the sacrifice of Christ: "the government shall be upon his shoulders." " I, saith he, bear up the pillars of it." These pillars rest upon Mount Calvary, and are strong to sustain his heritage, because they are moistened forever with the sacrifice of life. Hence, this kingdom shall never be destroyed. Because he lives, we shall live also; i. e. because he lives as the Lord of life, in virtue of his being the master and the destroyer of death, when he vacated its throne, and burst its cerements and terminated its gloomy reign; therefore we shall live also. On this foundation the church rests. It is•the sea of glass mingled with fire, on which the ransomed are gathered. If it were taken away, the church would be instantly destroyed; but the angels who never sinned would remain uninjured. They stand upon the merits of their own obedience, the saints upon the merits of Christ's obedience, and as he ever lives to make intercession, so his kingdom can never be destroyed. War and famine and pestilence may spread their ravages over whole countries; and voices, and thunderings, and lightnings, and great hail, may carry disaster every where, and fill whole kingdoms with lamentation, and mourning, and woe; yea, the sun may forget to shine, the earth forget to roll, the shock of death smite the centre of harmony and motion in the planetary system, and shake down the stars, and bury the material universe in the oblivious deep, from whence it originated; but no such disasters shall ever reach the kingdom of the Messiah. It is the bright spot in the centre of immensity and eternity, lifted up in striking contrast with the ruin that has marred the bowers of Eden, the temple of Zion, and the principalities in the heavenly places that kept not their first estate. Over it no cloud ever gathers, no thunder ever rolls; in it there is no more death, neither sorrow nor crying for the former things are passed away.

Thus we collect our testimony from prophets and apostles, from earth and heaven, against this restriction of the atonement to the mere permit to exercise pardon on the ground of divine sovereignty. This attenuated theory is not the atonement. It does not lift up the shadow of its palm upon the churches. It begins with spreading a robe over the whole world and ends with drawing its wasted shreds through the eye of a needle. This side of naked Unitarianism, there is no system more bald and meagre, more straitened and forbidding. Dr. Hodge characterizes it as "the parings of our system." It is singular that it should ever pass off for any thing more among Presbyterians. Yet still it has passed for more; for the gospel itself, and for the gospel entire. It has swept away the true theology and occupied its place with a famine of the bread of life. Like the lean kine, it has devoured the fat and well favored, and left us nothing but its own shadowy and hunger-bitten carcass.

Can it be said, that the atonement " does not of itself save a single soul?" The statement is a libel on the sacerdotal power and glory of him "who hath redeemed us to God by his blood." Can it be said that "all the atonement has effected for the sinner, is to place him within the reach of pardon." "It perfects forever by one offering all them that are sanctified."

To say, that "commutative justice was not satisfied, that the atonement paid no debt," is an error. Christ paid our debt of active obedience by his own, "by the obedience of one shall many be made righteous," bought us with his blood, "redeemed us to God by his blood," and delivered us from the debtor's poverty and from the debtor's prison. His blood has an appreciable value. It is heaven's high currency, is weighed in the balances of the sanctuary there, and its value cannot be gainsayed or made void. Foul indeed, must be the robe which has not been "washed and made white in the blood of the Lamb;" and poor and naked and ruined, the soul not invested with it. "Friend, how camest thou in hither not having on a wedding garment?"

To say that distributive justice is not satisfied, is an error. The atonement is both distributive and commutative. It is distributed to *every one* that believeth. The death that Jesus tasted was for *every son*. Faith appropriates him "as *our* Lord Jesus Christ," "made sin for *us*." The atonement was made for men, as individuals, and ends the demands of a law which distributes to every man according to his works, by distributing to him that very righteousness, demanded by the law. There is therefore, now no condemnation to them who are in Christ Jesus, for in him God hath condemned sin in the flesh, that the righteousness of the law might be fulfilled in us. Rom. 8. And as it is not made for some general distant metaphysical purpose, lying without the bounds of individual wants, and human sympathies, so *all* the saved must share as individuals in the gracious distribution. The ministerial commission authorizes us to say to each man, "he that believeth shall be saved, and he that believeth not shall be damned."

That "the penalty of the law, strictly speaking, was not

inflicted at all," is also incorrect. "Christ hath redeemed us from the curse of the law being made a curse for us." He satisfied the moral and ceremonial law and every kind of justice. There is no ingredient which can possibly enter into the nature of justice which he did not honor and satisfy. "The Lord is well pleased for his righteousness' sake, he will magnify the law and make it honorable." Isa. xlii. 21.

That the death of patriots and martyrs vindicates the main principle of atonement, is also erroneous. There are analogies, but they are found pre-eminently in the sacrifices of the Levitical law; under that law, the innocent and the guilty changed places and responsibilities, but these analogies strictly speaking, are not found in the whole history of friendship and patriotism and paternal love. Here we find self-denial, but self-denial is not "the main principle of atonement," or any principle of it. True it is, that Christ denied himself and it is equally so, that he was born and that he was crucified; and all this is likewise true of Peter, but was Peter crucified for us, or did he carry out a single principle of the atonement in his life or death? Surely not; he was a mere martyr.— But God sent forth his Son made of a woman, and made under the law, to redeem them that were under the law; and therefore the birth of Christ, the self-denial of his weary life and the agonies of the garden and of the cross, were all of the nature of atonement. If his humiliation had not been on "legal principles," it would not have partaken at all of the nature of atonement: he could not have redeemed us from the curse of the law, except as he was placed under it in our stead, and except, as his sufferings comprehended in them the curse of our sins. Aside from this fact, no sufferings of friends, patriots and martyrs can be said to partake of the nature of atonement, in the least degree. Where the law and justice of God are not somehow positively and truly satisfied there is no atonement. Christ hath suffered on legal principles, hath redeemed us from the curse of the law, being made a curse for us, and hath thereby exhibited and vindicated the entire principle of atonement, so that through the blood of the everlasting covenant we are made perfect to do his will. I conclude, therefore, that men who attempt to show how little Christ has done, and who speak of his work in the most depreciating manner, ought not to be regarded as being the great and almost only advocates of a full and sufficient propitiatory sacrifice.

That though, like the Unitarians, they attempt to hide their weakness by multiplying the consequences of the atonement in its fine impressions and grand results, yet so long as they deny that it includes in it an actual satisfaction to law and justice, and the actual and necessary redemption of every heir of glory, and maintain that the atonement cancels no demand, even for *one* man, nor saves a *single* soul, they do not relieve their system from the full and crushing weight of all the objections that fall upon it.

Great consequences grew out of the discovery of Moses by Pharaoh's daughter; and great consequences grew out of the sale of Joseph into Egypt; and also out of the treachery of Judas; yea, all events reach onward forever. As the motion of a finger vibrates along the whole atmosphere, so the most insignificant event may be felt far beyond the stars. But we are to do in this matter with the great and comprehensive fact of atonement, not alone with its incidental results. Did Christ die for our sins according to the Scriptures, and did he, by one offering, perfect forever all them that are sanctified? Are believers really redeemed from the curse of the law by Jesus Christ, or are they still under it? Is the law satisfied, or are its claims simply suspended by an act of divine sovereignty? These are the questions at issue; and so long as the New School deny that Christ obeyed unto death, as the legal representative of his people, so long their system must be regarded as substantially Unitarian.

The atonement destroys no man. As the ark, which was a type of it, was made to save, and drowned no one, so Christ came not to destroy men's lives, but to save them; to seek and to save the lost. Let the sinner flee to him: his sacrifice was not made to exclude, but to save men. It is not a rule, but a remedy. If you are lost, it will be by your own fault. This is their condemnation, that light is come into the world, and men have loved darkness rather than light, because their deeds are evil.

That the New School believe in the fullness of the atonement, and that the Old School do not, is to me a most singular misrepresentation. It is a great mistake: it completely changes the position of parties, and it is difficult to understand how it could ever gain currency in the Churches. Yet so it is: the very men who believe that Christ died sufficiently for all men, and distributively and effectually for the elect alone, are represented as denying the fullness of the atonement.

While those who do not believe that the atonement has any distributive relation whatever, or that "distributive justice is satisfied at all by it;" "that it does not consist in canceling the demand [even] for one man," or, "in itself save a single soul," are represented as believing in the fullness of the atonement: that Christ died for all men.

It is highly probable, however, that the false impression has been created by an improper use of terms in the controversy. The word *extent* has been used instead of the word *indefinite*. The latter term being the one which most exactly describes the New School opinions. They do not extend the atonement in its provisions, in the least degree beyond the bare possibility of pardon. "It rendered it not improper for the law-giver to pardon the transgressor." "It merely prepared the way for the proclamation of mercy." "It merely rendered pardon compatible." "It canceled no demand for one man, or all men." "It does not in itself save a single soul: it barely opens the door for the accomplishment of this object." Here is the boundary line; beyond this it does not *extend*. It does not reach (to use the catch phrases of the New Divinity) *commutative* or *distributive* justice, or the penalty of the law, or an individual soul. Restricted by its very nature, it is bound within narrow limits, by a law of necessity. "Oh, ye Corinthians, ye are not straitened in us: but ye are straitened in your own bowels."

"There is a third sense in which the term justice is frequently used, and the consideration of which will lead us directly to the nature of that satisfaction which Jesus Christ has made for sinners. We mean what is commonly denominated *general* or public justice. In order to distinguish it both from pecuniary and legal justice, it has been called moral justice. In this acceptation it has no direct reference to law, but embraces those principles of virtue or benevolence by which we are bound to govern our conduct, and by which God himself governs the universe." (Beman on Atonement, p. 132.) The satisfaction of Christ, according to this account of it, propitiates general or public justice; not pecuniary or legal justice, but moral justice; not a justice that has any direct reference to law, but it embraces the principles of virtue or general benevolence. Here, then, we are brought to an abyss, without form and void, where all correct distinctions are abandoned and confounded, where justice is made benevolence, and the atonement its manifestation,—where metaphysical fallacies gather their mists, and all that is substantial in the satisfaction of Christ vanishes into air.

The New School, then, do not extend the atonement: they limit and destroy it. Their general justice, which their atonement satisfies, has no existence, because no general person exists to whom it can belong, or toward whom it could be exercised. Justice is an attribute of God, every way definite and infinite; and the law is an institution which it creates and maintains, as it distributes to every man according to his works.

We are not bound to govern our conduct by some indefinite principles of benevolence, for there are no such principles; by the love of being in general, for there can be no such being to love; but by the law of God, from whose terrific curse we are delivered by a life of faith. The whole theory of disinterested benevolence, of general justice, and the love of being in general, is mere theory: it has amused and bewildered long enough. Its very friends begin to shun it, as one that is "'waxen poor, and fallen into decay." To say that the Redeemer satisfied its claims, is to say that he satisfied no claims whatever. It is not only to limit the atonement to a most insignificant point, to take away all that is full and definite and substantial in it, but to destroy it altogether.

When, therefore, the discussion originates between us and our opponents on the passage in Hebrews, "that he by the grace of God should taste death for *every* man," (Heb. ii. 9,) and on other similar passages, it is not a question as to the fullness of the atonement, but as to its definiteness, which is in debate. They contend for a meaning so universal as to include the whole race numerically, to show that Christ died as fully and as intentionally for Judas as for Paul; that his death relates as much to one man as to another; and that, therefore, it can have no definite relation to any man, because that view would result in Universalism: and that hence it was not a satisfaction "for *one* man or *all* men," but rather a manifestation of the evil of sin, and an impression in favor of virtue, or a governmental expedient.

We, on the contrary, maintain that the death of Christ was not a vague and indefinite transaction, but that it was endured for individual men,—includes in it the proper punishment of their sins, and includes in it also their inevitable redemption. Hence, it is that the New School, in contending for a general atonement, array themselves against those passages which declare it to be personal, distributive and efficient; and we are found, on the contrary, defending their plain and obvious meaning. "I lay down my life for the *sheep*." Christ "loved the *Church*, and gave himself for *it*;" was "made sin for *us*; was delivered for *our* offences;" "redeemed *us* from the curse of the law, being made a curse for *us*;" "is the end of the law to *every one* that that believeth." The Scriptures abound in passages of this kind, in which Christ is represented to have died for *men*, for *us*, for the *Church*; but I can find no passage in which it is said that his atonement does not of itself save a single soul, but that it *barely opens a door* to a possible pardon. That it opens such á door, we do not doubt. But this is not all which it effects; and the Scriptures no where countenance this restrictive and depreciating language to which the New School are obliged to resort in self-defence.

They also array themselves against all those Scripture testimonies which affirm that Christ suffered penally for us, and that justification is on legal principles. The text, "Christ hath redeemed us from the curse of the law, being made a curse for us," is a passage much in their way, because it states what Christ did in particular, beyond the bare opening of a door of hope in a general or indefinite way. That over and above this, he suffered penally and definitely for us, and that his sufferings were on legal principles,— were the curse of the law,— were an actual, an effectual, a completed redemption,— a redemption finished already by promise and by price,— and hence placed in its blessed results beyond the reach of every possible contingency. This text, therefore, they assail and torture, "and serve it as Saul of Tarsus did the early Christians; they compel it to blaspheme." And for the same reasons, the 53d chapter of Isaiah is made a perfect *auto da fe*. Here a whole group of witnesses are given over to the executioner. All the sacrifices of the law of Moses,—all the significancies of the priesthood,—all those passages in the 5th of Romans, on imputation, and all elsewhere on justification, are alike doomed by the inquisitors.

They array themselves also against all those numerous passages elsewhere which represent Christ as a *Redeemer*, and his blood as the price of redemption, by which he lifted the encumbrance from the forfeited patrimony, and by virtue of that full and sufficient price, puts every one of his impoverished kinsmen in full and final possession of their share in the estate. The blood of Christ is represented as a currency under the divine, as silver and gold are under the civil law. We are redeemed not with corruptible things, as silver and gold, but with the precious blood of Christ. But though the passages are very numerous, both in the Old and New Testaments, in which Christ the great Redeemer is represented as thus purchasing a possession, redeeming his people, and as having already paid the full price of their redemption on the cross. Yet they must all be assailed in like manner with the others, and it must be maintained that "the atonement paid no debt, canceled no demand for one man or all men," because, to admit it, would be to admit that Christ's death and precious blood-shedding has an inevitable efficiency in the salvation of his people; that it not only opened the door to pardon, but that it administers it, and justifies the soul, and opens the heart to receive Christ, and the grave to liberate the dead bodies of his saints, and the gate of glory to his ransomed people.— And as this would make too much of the atonement, so it becomes necessary to show that "the atonement paid no debt, canceled no demand." That to maintain such a view of the subject would be quite profane. "The august business which involved the honor of the divine government, the death of the Son of God, and the redemption of immortal man, is degraded to the level of a pecuniary transaction, is brought down to a mere matter of debt and credit. The declaration ought to be repeated, and the truth contained in it never forgotten, that commutative justice has nothing to do with the affair." (Beman on Atonement, p. 129.) Thus they fall upon the witnesses and attempt to slay them one by one.

But is it degrading to represent the atonement as paying a debt, when the Holy Ghost leads the way in the representation. And why cannot justice have debts of one kind as well as of another? if pecuniary claims are of the lower kind, that does not prove that there are no higher claims, which are as really demanded by justice to be liquidated as those claims that fix simply upon our silver and gold. If a man sold into slavery could be redeemed by gold, as the valuable consideration under the Jewish law, so may we be redeemed from bondage under the moral law, by the precious blood of Christ which is the valuable consideration paid for our ransom. I can see nothing degrading to God in this plain account given in the Scriptures of our redemption. There are surely other equivalents besides money. An eye may be taken for an eye, and a tooth for a tooth, as truly as one dollar for another. And there may be a debt for which no ransom short of blood shall be received. Thou shalt take no ransom for the murderers life. For whoso sheddeth man's blood by man shall his blood be shed.

Our lives were in this manner forfeited under the divine law. The inquiry had been made by the prisoners, "wherewithal shall I come before the Lord, and bow myself before the high God, shall I come before him with burnt offerings, with calves of a year old, will the Lord be pleased with thousands of rams or with ten thousands of rivers of oil? shall I give my first born for my transgression, the fruit of my body for the sin of my soul?" Micah. vi. 7, 8. But alas the price of redemption required by the law was greater than all these. It was the blood of the Son of God. No other could deliver, could redeem his brother, or give to God a ransom for him, no price less in value than this would suffice.

If the reader will carefully attend to the above passages in the word of God, and to the views of the two parties respecting their meaning, he will not fail to see that the nature of the atonement is the real point in debate. If we say Christ died to *save* men. They reply, he died to make salvation *possible.* If we say, he suffered the punishment due to our sins, they reply, he suffered no punishment at all.— If we say, he bought us with his blood and paid the price of our redemption ; this in their view degrades the atonement to the level of a pecuniary transaction. Indeed, so soon as we attempt to pass their *open door*—their *bare possibility* of pardon views—and begin to represent the Son as shedding forth the grace of effectual calling and final perseverance— as distributing the clean white linen, which is the righteousness of the saints; as purchasing and communicating a full and certain redemption, we at once encounter our New School brethren and find ourselves in the wide open field of debate and controversy. According to them, the atonement has no intrinsic efficiency whatever in our salvation. According to us it comprehends in it every particular in the entire redemption of the Church. The *one offering* not only opens the door but also perfects forever all them that are sanctified. All for whom Christ shed his blood upon the cross as the efficient price of their redemption shall in the dispensation of the fullness of time, wash their robes and make them white in the blood of the Lamb. None of them shall be found among the damned ; no one in that dark world of horror and despair, will ever claim that he was redeemed to God by the blood of Christ. His people shall never perish. Go, at the final consummation of all things into heaven, take up the book of life and read aloud every name which was contained on that vast muster roll of the King of Kings, " ere sin was born, or Adam's dust was fashioned to a man," and none of his redeemed shall fail to respond, He calleth his own sheep by name, he knoweth them that are his; he shall see the travail of his soul, and shall be satisfied; by his knowledge shall my righteous servant justify many, for he shall bear their iniquity."

The death of Christ comprehends in it absolutely all the redeemed, whether believers or not, whether already brought or of those he must yet bring, John x. 16; whether the much people he has in the city are already penitent or are still his enemies, Acts xviii. 10; whether already believers or of those who shall believe through the preached word. He hath loved them all with an everlasting love. John xvii. 20. The relationship has already been begun, by the susception on the part of the redeemer, of the flesh and blood of the children, with the full purpose of consumating the union thus established, by the inhabitation of his spirit, by imputing to them his righteousness, and by imparting to them his holiness; so that each one shall personally know the blessedness of that man, whose iniquities are forgiven, whose sins are covered. Not that the atonement, because thus distributed is therefore divided into parts, so much being appropriated to one, and so much to another, but each one needs a full atonement for *himself*, and has it all, and leaves it all to every other to be forever appropriated, and for ever used, and to remain forever undiminished and unchanged. As the light of day is appropriated by all, and remains to all the same, so Christ fills his own blessed kingdom, with his own "gracious fullness, to be appropriated by each, and to remain all, to all, without consumption and without end.

Our differences with the New School are not then as to the extent, but as to the fullness and definiteness of the atonement as a comprehensive and effective covenant transaction, we affirming, they denying, *we* making it a full redemption to God of all his people—*they* denying " that of itself it saves a single soul,"—we extending it to every particular in our redemption—they restricting it to a solitary point—we making it definite and personal respecting every one of the ransomed—they denying its personal relation to any man.

When therefore they contend that the atonement is indefinitely extended, we must understand them to mean that it is restricted to a definite and single point. When they contend that Christ died for every man, we must understand them to mean that he did not die for any man; when they maintain that Christ shed the blood of redemption for souls in hell, as well as souls in heaven; we are to understand that they intend to say hereby that his blood canceled no demand and saves no soul in heaven, earth or hell; that it is the surety of no covenant, but that our Lord died to satisfy the claims of a mental abstraction, called *general justice.*

This general justice is not the justice of God; for his justice is not *general* but a personal attribute inseparable from his very nature, and definite in its action rendering to every man according to his works. "General justice moreover has no direct reference to law," for legal justice is likewise personal. It takes hold upon the individual man for his personal delinquencies, saying, "pay me that *thou* owest." It curses "*every one*" that "continueth not in all things which are written in the book of the law to do them." Christ therefore, according the to New School, died to satisfy a justice which is not the justice of God, or the justice of his law.

To what being this public or general justice belongs, or whether to any being whatever, we are not told, as it is a very mysterious thing, living, in general every where, but gaining individuality no where; being neither an attribute of God, or of any other being, or belonging to any known law human or divine, so like all mysterious things, it is described by negatives. It is not commutative justice, nor distributive, it is not the justice of the law, it has no direct reference to that; it is general or public justice, i. e. it embraces those general principles of virtue or benevolence by which we are bound to regulate our conduct, and by which God governs the universe." We are bound to regulate our conduct by the law of God; as it is written, "Do we make void the law through faith? God forbid, yea we establish the law." This we can understand, but we are assured that this general justice has no direct reference to law. It is something else distinct from every thing which exists in God, in his law, or in his creatures, and this mere mental abstraction of which we can gain no notion and of which no one ever yet had a distinct idea, this is that personified nonentity which Christ died to satisfy: and when a general atonement is contended for, this is what we are to understand by it, viz: That it is indefinite with respect to the justice which it satisfies, for that is so *indefinite*, no one can tell us what it is, *indefinite* with respect to men, it has no relation to any man, *indefinite* with respect to its results, it secures nothing, saves no soul, opens an *indefinite* door of hope,—throws out an *indefinite* possibility of pardon and awakens an *indefinite* feeling of stupid wonder in all who hear of it. This is that unsubstantial, unscriptural view of the atonement against which we do most solemnly bear our testimony.

There are three views taken of the death of Christ, and these in reality comprise all others.

1. The CALVINISTIC: That Christ died *sufficiently* for all men, *efficiently* for the elect alone.

2. The UNIVERSALIST: That He died *sufficiently* and *efficiently* for all men.

3. The UNITARIAN: Which denies either *sufficiency* or *efficiency* to the death of Christ, and to this latter belong the New School views of the subject. In common with the Unitarians, they deny that Christ's obedience was vicarious, that his sufferings were penal, or that his death has in itself any efficiency in the matter of our redemption, and they maintain that man is not justified " by the righteousness of another, of God, or the Messiah," but by faith which is simply

an act of the mind "or a right heart," Here are all the elements essential to Unitarianism but *one*, that one relates to the doctrine of the Trinity, in every other essential particular, the two systems are strictly coincident and truly identical.

In these circumstances the controversy between Old and New School Presbyterians respecting the extent of the atonement is quite absurd. It would arise legitimately enough between us and the Universalists, whether such passages as state that Jesus "tasted death for every man," that "he is the propitiation for our sins and not for our ours only but for the sins of the whole world," that "he gave himself a ransom for all to be testified in due time," relate to a universal redemption of the human race, or whether they fairly admit of a different interpretation, but as between us and the New School, there can be no ground for debate respecting the extent of the atonement, our differences with them respect not its extent at all, but its nature and reality. Even our controversy with the old fashioned Hopkinsians, who hold a general atonement and a particular redemption, does not, strictly speaking, relate to the extent of the atonement, or to the fullness and sufficiency of the death of Christ as an effective purchase, but to the correctness of the distinction which they take between atonement and redemption. Our differences with all, then, on the atonement, except with the Universalists must relate not to its extent, but to its nature and reality. All, with this exception, limit the atonement in its saving benefits, to a part of the human race, as truly as we ourselves do, and hence I regard the time spent in discussing the question on the extent of the atonement with New School Presbyterians as time wasted on a false issue. We are called upon in this discussion, to defend the very doctrine of atonement itself, for this it is, which is assailed in its essential nature and its very existence wholly destroyed by the new divinity.

But if Christ died sufficiently for all men and efficiently for the elect alone, would not the nonelect believe a lie were they to believe that Christ died to save them? How then can you consistently call upon all men to believe on Christ? The reply is obvious. The first act of faith has respect to the sufficiency of the atonement to save the chief of sinners and whoever finds himself to be such is required to believe on Christ as the only Saviour of the ruined and the lost. This Christ Jesus truly is, the *only* and the *all sufficient* Saviour for the cheif of sinners : and no lost sinner filled with remorse and fear, and fleeing to Christ, could possibly believe a lie, were he to believe it with his whole heart. This belief moreover is of the nature of saving faith, the earliest exercise of this grace, and is the very thing required of the awakened and convinced sinner. Grace is always feeble in its beginings, "the bruised reed," "the smoking flax," the faintly defined parting line between daylight and darkness, are the inspired illustrations of its primary actings in the human heart. But when Christ shall have first been received, by one who thus esteems himself the chief of sinners, as the only and all sufficient Saviour of such, then after that he can rise to higher acts of faith, and at length attain unto its full assurance.

The argument of poor Joseph as related by Dr. Calamy, was the incipient demonstration of faith in its first struggles into life. Jesus Christ came to save the chief of sinners ; poor Joseph is the chief of sinners, therefore Jesus Christ came to save poor Joseph. "But what say you of your own heart, Joseph? Is there no token of good about it? No saving change there? Have you closed with Christ, by acting faith upon him?" "Ah no," says he, "Joseph can act nothing— Joseph has nothing to say for himself, but that he is the chief of sinners ; yet, seeing that it is a 'faithful saying' that Jesus he who made all things, came into the world to save sinners, why may not Joseph, after all, be saved?"

The change required in order to our salvation is not in the

nature of the atonement but in us. If by the spirit of God, we are led to renounce our own righteousness, and from a full and penitent conviction of our sin and misery, do trust in Christ alone for salvation, we shall be saved, whoever we may be, and whatever our guilt. "Whosoever shall call on the name of the Lord shall be saved." "Though your sins be as scarlet, they shall be as wool; red like crimson, they shall be as snow." Whoever, then, in the whole world, who possesses our common humanity, and perceives his guilt to be great, his depravity total, and that he must perish, without Christ, let him believe on him without hesitation; for such an one has all the qualifications of the publican, and him our Lord holds up for our imitation. Go, then, having these prerequisites, go into the presence of the Master, and smite upon your breast. We preach Christ crucified, "to the Jews, a stumbling-block; to the Greeks, foolishness, but to every one that believeth, the power of God and the wisdom of God." We venture on him as an all-sufficient Saviour. If all the sins of all men were our own, it would not weaken our confidence in his infinite ability, or if we had ten thousands souls to save, we should want no other arm to save than his who hung upon the tree. Were the load of our guilt heavier than the whole universe of material things, it would not break the grasp of his pity, or pluck us from the hand of his mediatorial power and grace.

But again: It is objected, that we are inconsistent, in making an indiscriminate offer of salvation to all men, forasmuch as we believe that the atonement is so perfectly discriminating, personal and definite. And to this we reply, that we never make an offer of salvation wholly indiscriminate. It is indiscriminate and indefinite with respect to the nations, communities and individuals addressed; but it is invariably and sufficiently discriminating in the very terms in which the offer is conveyed: "He that believeth shall be saved." The offer is here limited by the faith which it requires. "Christ is the end of the law for righteousness to every one that believeth." Here again the terms are definite. "Whosoever shall call on the name of the Lord shall be saved." Here also the terms of the offer define and limit it. The offers of salvation are never made to men respected simply as unbelievers, or as those who shall remain such, but invariably have respect to the grace of faith, which they suppose or require; and they are in no instances made to any man, without this accompanying limitation, either expressed or implied. Believe, then, on the Lord Jesus Christ, and thou shalt be saved.

But how can the New School make the offer of salvation to any man, since, according to them, he did not die for any man, but for some other purpose. If a man should believe that Christ died for the chief of sinners, and, therefore, for him, and that, because he finds himself to be the chief of sinners, would he not, then, believe a lie, since Christ did not die for any sinner, as such? Would he not believe a lie, were he to believe that Christ redeemed him from the curse of the law? since, "though a thousand substitutes should die," the claims of the law could never be invalidated; and since, as Christ did not bear the curse of the law, so he could bring no one out from under it? If the sinner were to receive Christ as the end of the law for righteousness to every one that believeth, would he not receive an imposter to his arms; inasmuch "as the sufferings of Christ have no direct reference to law, but to those general principles of virtue or benevolence," which are the attributes of no being, and belong to no law, human or divine?

How, then, can the New School, with the least show of consistency or propriety, offer the atonement distributively to every man, since distributive justice is not satisfied by it, and since it was not made for man as an individual, and since it is not true, that Christ tasted death "for one man, or all men?" There can be no truth in the offer; for he offers to a sinner an atonement not made for him. There can be no sincerity in the offer; for he knows, when he makes it, that the atonement was made for something he calls general justice, and not for the sinner. There can be no use in the offer; for he offers (when he comes to explain himself,) really nothing. The sinner is not under general justice,—has not offended general justice, and seeks no deliverance from this personified nonentity. He is under the law of God. This law he has broken: from its curse, he would be freed; and, if the New School atonement has no direct reference to this law, then the convinced sinner can have no direct interest in hearing any thing about it. He is in a particular difficulty with the law and justice of God: All here is definite and terrible; and he needs an atonement that will meet definitely his wants, and deliver him from the pollution of his sin, and from the misery of his condemnation. The gospel we preach meets precisely his wants; but when the New School attempt to preach Christ on the indefinite principle, no one can understand what they mean. As their views are indefinite, so their preaching is indefinite, and the impression created is indefinite; and the bewildered worshippers are in the dilemma of Mary, when she sought her murdered Lord. He was taken away, and she could not tell where they had laid him. She had gone to the wrong place to find him: he was not in the sepulchre any more, nor yet is he to be found any more in the matured New School divinity. Those who seek him there, seek for him in vain. The alarm felt on the part of godly Presbyterians, scattered among the New School, increases daily. They are beginning to hear "a voice behind them, saying, This is the way; walk ye in it." "Thus saith the Lord, Stand ye in the way, and see, and ask for the old paths, where is the good way?" The old paths are becoming more and more obvious,—the way of escape more and more plain. Duty to God and his cause, to themselves and their families, will lead them back again to the bosom of the Presbyterian Church, from whence they have been decoyed. The day, I believe, is not far distant, when their eyes shall be fully opened, and when they shall make their escape from these pestilent errors. May the great Head of the Church bless his people, and lift them up forever. AMEN.

CHAPTER V.

DOCTRINAL DIFFERENCES CONTINUED.

Natural depravity—Denied by the New School—Its importance—Its denial dangerous.

In John iii. 7, it is said: "Ye must be born again." Must, is emphatic in this sentence, it being the intention of our Lord to assert the necessity of regeneration, as it is created by the positive contrariety of man's moral nature to that of God's. "That which is born of the flesh is flesh, and that which is born of the spirit is spirit. Marvel not that I said unto thee, Ye *must* be born again." A sinful nature unites with sinful objects; a holy nature with holy objects. Their affinities are opposite. Flesh is flesh,—unites with it, and resists, with its entire tendencies, the spirit. Spirit unites with spirit, and resists, with its entire tendencies, any union with flesh. Those differences which lie in the very nature of the things themselves, are the greatest possible; and such are the differences which actually separate unregenerate man from God. These differences are in man's moral nature. This is very clear, not only from the 3d of John, but from many other passages of inspiration. From among these, I select one, in Rom. viii. 7, 8: "Because the carnal mind is enmity against God; for it is not subject to the law of God, neither indeed can be. So then they that are in the flesh cannot please God." This statement is sufficiently definite and positive. No sentence could be constructed which could more fully corroborate the view I have taken.

The impossibility is absolute. The moral nature of unrenewed man, and the moral nature of the ever-blessed God, are positive enmities; and, if left to the uninterrupted election of their own opposite affinities, the separation between them is hopeless and endless. Fire can unite with fire, and increase the reciprocal heat. Water can unite with water, and swell its kindred drops into seas; but, constituted as they are, they resist, with destructive violence, all union with each other. If it were even possible, by some new chemical combination, to modify, in some degree, their mutual antagonisms; yet it could not be true of sin and holiness, flesh and spirit, the carnal mind and the law of God. No new natural combinations can ever destroy, or even modify, the total and infinite enmity,—whatever may have been the intellectual and moral culture received by the carnal mind. However strikingly it may have simulated every virtue and every grace, it is still enmity against God. And the absolute impossibility remains. "They that are in the flesh cannot please God."

Presbyterians, accordingly, believe that "the sinfulness of that estate whereinto man fell, consists in the guilt of Adam's first sin; (see the explanation and defence of this point in the first part of the 3d chapter;) the want of original righteousness, together with the corruption of his whole nature, which is commonly called original sin." Original righteousness is wanting in fallen man. In his primeval state, the possession of it was his perfection and his glory. It was the image of God,—a mirror on which he lifted up the light of his countenance, and in which reposed a miniature resemblance of himself,—his own image in knowledge, righteousness, and true holiness. Regeneration is the restoration of that image in its inception. Man in it is "renewed in knowledge, righteousness, and true holiness, after the image of Him that created him," and begins to wear, in some small degree, the early glory of his nature. When our first parent fell, this original righteousness was lost to the race: "In Adam all die." God departed, withdrew his image, and left the soul in moral ruins. As the setting sun leaves the earth in darkness, not by shedding darkness upon it, but by withdrawing ois beams, so God left the soul in sin, not by infusing sin into it, but by withdrawing from it, its original righteousness. The law required this righteousness in all created intelligences; and whenever it was wanting in man, he fell into all evil.

This privation of original righteousness was the point at which commenced the corruption of his whole nature, — "whereby he was utterly indisposed, disabled, and made opposite to all that is spiritually good, and wholly inclined to all that is evil, and that continually." His mind, losing all its high and holy affinities, became at once carnal, and enmity against God. It was no longer subject to his law, and, indeed, it never can be, but by an act of creation as difficult and as wonderful as that which created his original righteousness. God, who created it, took it from him, and he alone can restore it, when the sinner is "born, not of blood, nor of the will of the flesh, nor of the will of man, but of God. John i. 13.

Depravity is called natural, because it is conveyed by ordinary generation. That which is born of the flesh is flesh. John iii. 6. Children are like their parents in their whole nature, body and soul, tendencies and developments. "Behold, I was shapen in iniquity, and in sin did my mother conceive me." Ps. li. 5. "Who can bring a clean thing out of an unclean?" Job xiv. 4. Shall clean animals, as sheep and kine, proceed from wolves and hyenas? The law that binds each distinct race to itself is uniform and universal. In the vegetable kingdom every plant, and every shrub, and every tree multiplies from itself, and after itself; the original germ lives, and bears, and spreads every where, after its own kind. Throughout the whole animal kingdom, the same law prevails; like produces like; all the races, in all ages, retain their original natures, and are preserved from amalgamation by necessity. The first remove is the last which it is possible to make; the unnatural variety is barren. Their very characteristics are propagated with a marked uniformity and universality. Not only the muscle and form of the lion and tiger, but the courage of the one, and the cruelty of the other, are equally common and striking evidences of their origin and nature. Man is not an exception to this uniform and universal law, which governs the progress and propagation of every living thing besides. He begets a posterity in his own likeness: his body and soul, his whole nature physical and intellectual, social and moral, is contained in the first man, and it multiplies itself from generation to generation. "He hath made [them] of one blood." "He fashioneth their hearts alike." The making and the fashioning belong to both body and mind. The infant child possesses the carnal mind of its parent, when first it lives and breaths, as truly as when in subsequent manhood, it embodies its enmity in words and actions. The lion's whelp, harmless and impotent to destroy in the period of its incipency, is, nevertheless, a lion still.— All is there, which afterwards renders him terrible to both man and beast, when he "roars after his prey, and seeks his meat from God." The same is true of man. The infant is the yet immature, but real enemy of God. Maturity, only, is needed to prove him earthy, sensual, devilish; thus, the doctrine of native depravity is fully sustained, by all the analogies in nature, meets us every where, in the whole world, in every living thing. In the hour of calm and unbiassed reflection, the belief of it, forces itself upon our soberest convictions. It is clearly taught in the word of God. But, if revelation had been wholly silent on the subject, yet it is so obvious, the evidence of it lies around us in such vast profusion, it would require a special revelation to induce a contrary belief. No one would be able to show why the human race should prove an exception to a rule otherwise universal.

Yet the New School have adopted a different view of this whole subject. "Neither a holy nor a depraved nature are possible without understanding, conscience, and choice. To say of an accountable creature, that he is depraved by nature, is only to say, that rendered capable by his maker of obedience, he disobeys from the commencement of his accountability." (See sermon on the native character of man, by Dr. Beecher.) "Is only to say," what the Dr. does not say; it is in fact to contradict expressly and in the very next breath his own statement, to take back his own words; to declare that that which is natural is merely voluntary, and not natural; that the water in the fountain is bitter, that is to say, the stream from it is bitter, but the fountain itself is sweet, it is not bitter. "It is a question alike pertinent and important, whether in the incipient period of infancy and childhood, there can be any moral character whatever possessed, * * * properly speaking we can predicate of it neither sin nor holiness." (Duffield on Regeneration, pp. 377. 399.) But the question is, in my judgement, as improper as the conclusion is incorrect. There can be no pertinency in questioning a revealed fact, nor propriety in denying it.

Mr. Barnes remarks, in his Notes on Romans, v. 14: "The passage here states a great and important principle, that men will not be held to be guilty, unless there is a law which binds them, of which they are apprized, and which they voluntarily transgress." "If it should be said that the death of infants would prove that they were sinners also, I answer, (a) that this was an inference which the Apostle does not draw, and for which he is not responsible. It is not affirmed by him. (b) If it did refer to infants, what would it prove? Not that the sin of Adam was imputed, but that they were personally guilty and transgressors." But infants surely, are not apprised of the law of God, neither can they voluntarily transgress it. And as according to Mr. Barnes, knowledge of the law, is essential to guilt, so is it also to holiness. Infants then have no moral character whatever. They are neither good nor bad. They are mere animals. This last it is true, is an inference, which Mr Barnes does not draw; yet it is legitimate, and for it, his system is responsible. Mr. Barnes after rejecting every other explanation of Rom. v. 19; "By one man's obedience many were made sinners;" and almost conceding all a presbyterian could wish on native depravity, finally throws off the mask, and from the 8th Rem. to the end of his remarks on that verse, defends the Unitarian explanation. "The facts here stated accord with all the analogies in the moral government of God. The drunkard secures as a result commonly that his family will be reduced to beggary, want and woe. A pirate or a traitor will whelm not himself only, but his family in ruin. Such is the great law or constitution on which society is now organized, and we are not to be surprized that the same principle occurred in the primary organization of human affairs." * * * "If it exists now it existed then." * * * "The doctrine should be left therefore simply as it is in the Scriptures. It is there the simple statement of a fact without any attempt at explanation." * * * * "How this is, the Bible has not explained; it is a part of a great system of things."

The Bible, however, does explain how depravity is conveyed; it is by "ordinary generation." "I was shapen in iniquity, and in sin did my mother conceive me." "That which is born of flesh is flesh." "And were by nature, children of wrath." In these and similar passages, the explanation of the manner in which depravity is conveyed, finds melancholly utterance, but nevertheless, that explanation is clear, direct and sufficient. Mr. Barnes, however, has no eye to see it, no ear to hear it. It meets *him* every where; but *he* meets it no where, and his profound reverence for the Scriptures, leads him to discourage all attempts at the explanation of a fact, whose only obscurity and mysteriousness, have their origin in his singular denial of its existance. Then, as is usual with him, in similar dilemmas, he furnishes an explanation as unsound as it is, laboured and unsatisfactory, and that also, after solemnly assuring us that it "should be left simply as it is in the Scriptures, it is there the simple statement of a fact without any attempt at explanation." * * "The drunkard secures commonly as a result that his family shall become beggard, and the pirate and traitor whelm themselves and families in ruin; such was the primary organization of human affairs." Such is the explanation of a fact, by Mr. Barnes, in regard to which the Scriptures according to him, are silent, and where we should all reverently leave it, to its repose, without any attempt at explanation.

We are to understand then, that as the families of drunkards and pirates are not drunkards and pirates by nature, but by the corrupting influence of a bad example; that as a different education would have secured a different result, and that as this is the great constitution under which we are placed; therefore, depravity proceeds not from a bad nature, but from a "social liability." This is precisely the faith of Unitarians. "It is not the depravity of nature in which we believe. Human nature, nature as it exists in the bosom of an infant, is nothing else but capability. Capability of good as well as evil. The more likely from its exposures to be evil than good. It is not depravity then, but the depravation of nature in which we believe." (Dr. Dewey's Controversial Discourses, p. 18.) Such strikingly evident coincidences in opinion, between Mr. Barnes and the Unitarians, led one of their writers in the Christian Examiner, to say in his review of Mr. Barne's notes: "That while our orthodox brethren publish and circulate, and receive with favor, such books as these, we most cordially extend to them the right hand of fellowship." And, indeed, I can perceive no substantial differences between Mr. Barnes and his liberal friends on the subject of native depravity. This I admit would not of necessity prove his views erroneous, but it would prove that they were not presbyterian.

The system of Mr. Finney also is a kindred drop in the sea of error. "All depravity is voluntary, consisting in voluntary transgression; Oh, the darkness and confusion and utter nonsense of that view of depravity, which exhibits it as something lying back, and the cause of all actual transgression. (See sermon on important subjects p. 139.)

The New School then, believe that children are depraved when they knowingly and willfully violate the commands of God. Back of this period, according to them, moral distinctions cannot obtain. Many of the New School hold with Dr. Dewey that in infancy there is simple capability to good and evil. But Mr. Barnes admits an antecedent certainty, Rom. v. 19. "There is something antecedent to the moral action of his (Adams) posterity and growing out of the relation which they sustain to him, which makes it certain that they will sin as soon as they begin to act as moral agents." "The renewed man is exposed to temptation from his strong native appetites, and the power of these passions strengthed by long habit before he was converted, has traveled over into religion and distress him." Rom vii. 14. "A man who was an infidel before his conversion, and whose mind filled with skepticism, and cavils, and blasphemy, will find the effects of his former habits of thinking, lingering in his mind, and annoying his peace for years." Rom. vii. 15. And verse 19; "in his heart, and conscience, and habitual feeling, he did not choose to commit sin, but abhorred it." And verse 18; "The obstacles are not natural, but such as arise from long indulgence in sin, the strong native propensity evil."

Among the New School, these two opinions prevail. The first is, that infants are equally capable of good or evil, and yet, always sin as soon as they become moral agents. It is sufficient to say of this opinion, that it contains the doctrine of a uniform effect, without a sufficient cause. If it maintained, that moral beings, capable of good and evil, had been sometimes good and sometimes evil, it would change its aspect of absurdity. It is the uniformity and universality of sin among all men. The want of a single exception for six thousand years, and the admitted certainty, that there never will be an exception, which mocks at this opinion. If it be urged that Adam fell and that angels fell; I reply, Adam also obeyed for a season, and holy angels obey still. In these instances the capabilities work in both directions, but in this they forever work in one direction only. In every instance, in every age, under all circumstances, the first moral act is invariably evil when it could as well have been good. The opinion cannot be correct; it not only contradicts revelation, but aside from that consideration, it wears the air of a total improbability.

The opinion that something prior to moral action makes it certain that our first moral acts will be evil, is a more plausible account of our depravity. But to say that that something is not itself sinful, involves an absurdity of another kind, equally great with the former. That mental state which makes sin inevitable, must be in its own nature sinful, even more sinful, than the sinful acts themselves that proceed from it. These acts are transient, leave their stain, and pass away. But their source is permanent, and embosoms and issues them all. It is the father of lies, and the mother of abominations. It makes the throat an open sepulcher, and the feet swift to shed blood. It gives the tongue to evil, and pours the poison of asps under the lips. It fills the eyes with adultery, and blinds them to the fear of God. It must therefore be sin; sin in its concentrated odiousness, vitality, and strength; the giant sin among the sins of men. The serpents poison is in his tooth, he carries it with him, even when he does not bite. He may never kill, yet he has enough in store to slay thousands; this makes him dreadful, and arms the world against his life. Our actual transgressions are many but they appear not in infancy, and they are intermitted when we faint or while we sleep. But the sin of nature is an inexhaustable poison always with us and ready on every occasion and is the principle cause of the wrath of heaven. The grapes of Sodom are bitter, but the vine of Sodom is principally in fault. ." Make the tree good and the fruit will be good. Do men gather grapes of thorns, or figs of thistles?" "Oh, Israel, wash thy heart from wickedness how long shall thy vain thoughts lodge within thee." "For from within, from the heart of man, proceed evil thoughts, adulteries, fornications, murders, thefts, covetousness, wickedness, deceit, laciviousness, an evil eye, blasphemy, pride, foolishness."— "Create in me a clean heart, Oh, God." Maternal love is the same whether it be in a state of activity or in a state of repose. Evil thoughts are the activities of an evil heart and they are both alike evil. All actions good or bad are not only so in themselves, but in their source. We judge of the one by the other. That something in the soul, which makes us sin, is itself sinful, the two possess a common character and give complexion to each other. To deny this, softens no stern feature of truth, removes no difficulty out of the way in understanding it; but introduces an error which contradicts the word of God, is at variance with all analogy and confounds the distinctions between good and evil.

The belief in native depravity promotes repentance and humility. Its denial hardens the heart. David had committed two great evils, but they were only drops of bitterness, compared with the fountain itself. That fountain must be healed, or all was lost. He would confess his sin,—the great sin, the sin of nature, the one most odious and most to be dreaded. "I was shapen in iniquity, and in sin did my mother conceive me." He would prevent another fall, but that he never could prevent, while the sin of nature reigned; its power must be broken. "Create in me a clean heart, O

God." His views of native depravity filled him with self-loathing, and brought him to God for help. He could indulge in no views of self-complacency. He had grieved away the spirit, and his fall was nature, unrestrained, unassisted nature, acting out its desperate wickedness. The restoration of the Holy Spirit, for which he prayed, was not only necessary to his mental peace, but to his future safety. The adversary, that had reigned within, was too mighty for man's unaided strength. Hence his prayer, — "Uphold me by thy free spirit." Had he rejected the doctrine of native depravity, he could have said, These evil deeds are the result of a strong temptation, not of a bad nature. And he could have felt, as all bad and blinded mortals usually do, that his actions had been sinful, but still he was good at heart, and was not naturally destitute of purity and humanity.

Paul, when he would awaken among the Ephesians emotions of humility and gratitude, assures them, that they were quickened when dead in sin, and that they were, by nature, children of wrath. They were delivered from something more than a life of impiety and immorality. These were but the effects of a cause far more dark and damning; and the gteatness of the disease enhanced the greatness of the cure. Evil habits might be broken off, but nature could not cure its sinful tendencies; this was the work of grace alone, and must awaken, in the highest degree, both their humility and gratitude. The qualifying language of Mr. Barnes, — "He did not use, he did not say [*Phusei,*] 'By birth, or before you were converted.' * * * * I do not affirm when you began to be such, or that you were such as soon as you were born; * * whether by a corrupted soul, or by imputed guilt; whether you act as a moral agent as soon as you were born, or at a certain period of childhood. I [Paul] do not say." (Barnes' Notes, Eph. ii. 3.) Such ideas were not in Paul's mind; such language was not to his purpose.

It was not the habit of the Apostle to say one thing and mean another,—to say that they were, by birth, the children of wrath, and not mean what he said. He was not afraid of leading the Ephesians to carry their moral distinction too far back, even to the very origin of their being; for it was the very thing he did, and intended to do,—the very fire with which he would kindle their gratitude,—the very climax at which he aimed in his eloquent contrast.

Nicodemus was an awakened and inquiring sinner, but he was not told that he had sinned from the commencement of moral agency, and that his nature needed no change; that he had but to change his principles, objects, and pursuits,—an affair of no great difficulty, and within his power at any moment. There was no softening of the terrible aspect of things now gathering in gloom around the stricken-hearted ruler of the synagogue. But he was assured that, above and beyond his saddest revery, was his necessity great, and his condition dreadful. He was born of the flesh, and was flesh. Nature and habit both united him to evil; he sought it as sparks go upwards, or as water flows from the fountain, and seeks its accustomed channel. That the birth which he needed was of the Holy Ghost, and this alone could commence his return to God.

Saul of Tarsus never fully closed with Christ till he was wholly persuaded of his total depravity by nature. Then he could say, "I know that in me, that is in my flesh dwelleth no good thing. I was alive without the law once, [O! dreadful life of a most deplorable darkness and spiritual insensibility!] but when the commandment came, sin revived and I died." The sin of nature did not appear sin before. It dwelt in him, and he knew it not, but aroused now into life, it appeared sin, and wrought in him all manner of concupisance. The instructions of inspired men are nowhere on this subject apologistical and explanatory. They did not draw out the spirit's naked blade, and then amuse their audiences by an exhibition of their skill in breaking it in pieces before their eyes. Native depravity was hell's dark citadel in the heart of man. A conviction of its existence was necessary to saving repentance and faith. They knew it themselves, and others must know it, or be lost. Their attack was open and direct. They gave utterance to a truth which oppressed them with alarm for the safety of their hearers. They sang no syren song to lull men into a feeling of false security, amid the shoals and breakers of the sea of Sodom. Theirs was the midnight cry! It struck a chord whose vibrations went to the inmost soul, and convinced sinners came trembling and astonished, and said,— Sirs, what must we do to be saved? Can it be said, then, that our differences with the New School are merely philosophical, relating only to the mere theory of religion? What! when we teach, and you believe, that your nature must be changed before your actions can be acceptable to a holy God? can it be of no account whether we are followed by commentators and ministers who affirm that our habits are bad, our conduct sinful, but that our nature is not itself depraved? If our instructions were correct, were leading you to repentance, to prayer, to faith, then theirs would lead you back again into your former state of false security, away from the spirit's regeneration, and from a Saviour's bleeding side.

These erroneous teachings meet and embarrass us at every point. It was a maxim of Luther, that the Scriptures could not be understood but by a portion of that spirit by which they were originally inspired. It is taught by us, that man wants his original knowledge, as well as righteousness, and true holiness. It is taught by the Apostle, that "the natural man deserneth not the things of the spirit of God,—neither can he know them; for they are spiritually discerned;" (1 Cor. ii. 14;) that the "understanding of man is darkened, and that he is alienated from the life of God, through the ignorance that is in him, because of the blindness of the heart." Eph. iv. 18. And if, under these instructions, your perceived impotence and awakened fears lead you to cry to Him that "commandeth the light to shine out of darkness, to shine into your hearts, to give you the light of the knowledge of the glory of God as it is in the face of Jesus Christ. 2 Cor. iv. 6. How most unhappy would be the effect, if you were to read and believe the following statement from Mr. Barnes on the same proof texts,—Eph. iv. 18: It is not that God has enfeebled the human intellect, by a judicial sentence, on account of the sin of Adam, and made it incapable of perceiving the truth; it is not that there is any deficiency or incapacity of natural powers; it is not that the truths of religion are so exalted that man has no natural ability to understand them; for they may be as well understood as any other truths. * * It follows, too, that as man has debased his understanding by sin, it is needful to make an exertion to elevate it again; hence, the necessity of schools at missionary stations." When we assert the inability of the understanding, he asserts its ability. When we present to you the divine teacher in his immediate and subjective illumination, he presents to you a company of ministers and school teachers. When we point you to the Holy Ghost, whose office-work it is to take the things of Christ and show them unto you, and endeavor to bring you near, that you may read and hear amid the attractive and subduing effulgence which he sheds upon the understanding and the heart. Mr. Barnes interposes with a lens of ice, and chills the warm current of the soul, by assuring us "that divine truths are not so exalted that man has not natural ability to understand them, and hence the necessity of schools at missionary stations."

But whether the understanding or the conscience, the will or the affections, are made the subjects of examination, the result is the same. Native depravity is denied to exist in the soul, or in any faculty of the soul. You will find these denials summarily presented in Mr. Barnes' Notes on 2 Cor. viii. 12. "He requires a service strictly according to our ability, and to be measured by that. He demands no more than our powers are fitted to produce, no more than we are able to render. Our obligations in all cases are limited by our ability. This is obviously the rule of equity, and this is all that is anywhere demanded in the Bible, and this is everywhere demanded. Thus our love to him is to be in proportion to our ability, and not to be graduated by the ability of angels, or other beings." "And thou shalt love the Lord thy God with all thy heart, and with all thy soul, and with all thy mind, and with all thy strength." Mark xii. 30. "Here the obligation is limited by the ability, and the love is to be commensurate with the ability. So of repentance, faith, and of obedience in any form. None but a tyrant can demand more than can be rendered,—and to demand more is the appropriate description of a tyrant, and cannot appertain to the ever-blessed God." The above precept quoted by Mr. Barnes, from Mark xii. 30, cannot be to his purpose, unless it is a question already settled in his mind, that a change of heart by the Holy Ghost is unnecessary previously to the exercise of holy affections; that the heart is good enough as it is, and needs not to await the work of the Holy Ghost upon it, in order to holy love; that the moral nature of man is all right in itself, wrong only in its exercises and habits ; these are under our own control, and we can change them at our pleasure. For if he intended to maintain that God did for man in regeneration what he could not do for himself; that a change, inward, spiritual and supernatural, must necessarily precede all holy exercises, then all he has said about ability is mere rhapsody. But if he intended to deny the necessity of such a change altogether, then he is at least consistent with himself, but alas! he is at war with the word of God, and with the faith of his people.

Mr. Barnes in his notes on 3d chapter of John, appears to hold a different view of this subject. But I find there, a reference to his notes on John xiv. 4. and here again he appears quite correct. But I am still referred for further explanation to Rom. v. 19. and here the mask drops, and (from his 8th note to the end, which see) he fully explains himself. The text in 2 Cor. viii. 13. however, is a favorite one with men of this class. Mr. Finney having asserted that the Bible was full of the doctrine of plenary natural ability ; finally, makes one quotation in proof of it, and that proof is this same text in 2 Cor. " For if there be first a willing mind it is accepted according to that a man hath, and not according to that he hath not." Indeed, this is the only passage in the Bible, on which they seem to rely. Elsewhere the Bible is full of the doctrine of natural depravity and human impotence. " We are without strength." Rom. v. 6. " Not that we are sufficient of ourselves to think any thing as of ourselves, but our sufficiency is of God. 2. Cor. iii. 5. " For the flesh lusteth against the spirit, and the spirit against the flesh, and these are contrary the one to the other so that ye cannot do the things that ye would." Gal. v. 7. The carnal mind is enmity against God ; for it is not subject to the law of God, neither indeed can be. Rom. viii. 7. The natural man discerneth not the things of the spirit of God, neither can he know them, for they are spiritually discerned. 1 Cor. ii. 1. " No man can come unto me except the Father, who hath sent me, draw him." John vi. 44. " Without me ye can do nothing." John xv. 15. " Except a man be born again he cannot see the kingdom of God." John iii. 3. Thus the testimony is not a solitary drop oozing out reluctantly from a violently compressed sponge, but it breaks around us in the swellings of Jordon.

The Scriptures are consistent with themselves, and the passage in 2 Cor. viii. 12, is not a contradiction of their current testimony. It does not deny native depravity at all, nor does it assert that man is able to obey God without a previous change in his moral nature. If we should grant that the doctrine is contained in the Bible, it surely is not contained in this text. The text simply states a rule of duty among Christians, to regulate them in their charitable contributions. And the rule is applicable to all Christians in all their services. They are accepted in the beloved ; " they are not under the law but under grace." God " beholds no iniquity in Jacob, and no perverseness in Israel." And because he accepts his people who are not under the law, and does not require of them as a condition of acceptance perfect obedience to it, an obedience which they were not able to render ; does it hence follow, that the same rule applies to the unrenewed who are still under the law ? It cannot be. Believers make the law their rule, but do not make perfect obedience to its precepts the condition of their acceptance. From that bondage they are delivered. Under it, all others are held ; and except they believe in Christ will be required to do what it is impossible for fallen man to do— to keep it perfectly, or perish under its curse. Faith in Christ is the only remedy, because obedience to the law is a perfect impossibility. " For if there had been a law given which could have given life, verily righteousness should have been by the law." Gal. iii. 21. Dr. Duffield maintains that the sinner is not utterly unable by his own unassisted powers either to believe or repent to the saving of his soul, (and that) it might as truly be said that he cannot rise up and walk by his own unassisted powers. (vide Duffield on Regeneration p. 342.) And Mr. Finney maintains " that if the sinner ever has a new heart, he must obey the commandment in the text and make it himself." (Sermons on important subjects, pp. 18 to 38.) Now, on a most careful examination and comparison of the views of the New School, of Mr. Finney, and of the Unitarians on this subject, I am fully convinced that they are *one*. Not indeed in their philosophy and methods of defence ; but *one* in their results. They all by their different routs arrive at the same conclusion, viz : that the doctrine of the natural moral depravity of man is a mere figment, and the necessity of regeneration by the Holy Ghost, in order to holy obedience, the idle philosophy of the schools.

These errors are of a very serious and dangerous character. Wherever they prevail, they dry up the fountains of repentance, quench the life of faith, and harden the hearts of men. No true and great work of grace can be expected to commence until they are exposed and rejected. They array themselves like Judeism against the gospel. Not as they are an organized system of persecution, but an organized system of false opinions. They are more disguised than Unitarianism. Yet equally a denial of man's ruin by the fall and equally opposed to the spirits glory and work. They are the tares of the field, which must be ploughed under. The teeth of the dragon sown broadcast on the churches, they must be ground to powder. We are no lovers of controversy; but we have reached a point where forbearance is no longer a virtue, necessity is laid upon us, and for Zion's sake, and Jerusalem's sake we cannot hold our peace. When Paul would promote true religion, he also assailed the false. He disputed in the school of one Tyrannus ; he disputed with the Stoics and philosophers and Judeaizing teachers, and insisted in opposition to their views upon the truths of Christianity. In like manner we feel called upon to dispute this whole system of theological error, and "philosophy falsely so called." To declare to you that depravity is natural and regeneration essential. A change in objects and pursuits or in governing purposes will be of no avail. A supernatural change must pass upon your moral nature. " Do men gather grapes of thorns or figs of thistles?" " Make the tree good and the fruit will be good." That which is born of the flesh is flesh ; its work is manifest fornication, uncleanness, witchcraft, hatred, variance, emulations, wrath, strifes, seditions, heresies, envyings, murders, drunkeness, revelings. Its nature is manifest, hatred, wrath, heresies, envyings, belong not to the animal propensities but to the moral nature of man, and show us what that nature is. Its true character cannot be mistaken. Listen not then to smooth and flattering words, believe not that there is no danger; that there is no such dreadful depravity, deep, damning and universal, bearing a ruined world to a sea of fire; listen not to those, who cry peace, when there is no peace; ability when there is no ability. Freedom from the the depravity of nature, when its abiding taint dries up your marrow, throbs along every artery, and gathers a film on the eye of reason, and turns the manly brow to brass, and the heart to an adamant stone. These sad results are not the results of a bad example but of a bad nature. Not inveterate because habitual, but inveterate and habitual and universal, because they are natural. "Who can bring a clean thing out of an unclean." That which is born of flesh is flesh. "Verily, verily I say unto thee, except a man be born again he cannot see the kingdom of God," (John iii. 3.) neither here nor hereafter, "for there shall in no wise enter into it any thing that defileth, neither any thing that worketh abomination or maketh a lie." Rom. xxi. 29. Let no man deceive you with vain words for because of these things cometh the wrath of God on the children of disobedience. Eph. v. 6.

CHAPTER VI.

DOCTRINAL DIFFERENCES CONTINUED.

The despensation of the Spirit—The New School by their views of ability and depravity, make the Spirits despensation void—They make truth an agent.—The Spirit the only agent in regeneration—They place infants on a level with mere animals.

The necessity of the spirit's renovating agency has its foundation in natural depravity. In the beginning the earth was without form and void, and darkness was on the face of the deep; and in this condition it would have remained forever, but for the interposition of Him who created all things for himself. The fall broke in upon the laws of harmony and motion in the moral world, precipitated it into a second chaos, in which its early beauties were blighted, and its glory lost. And in this state it must forever have remained, except " He who commanded the light to shine out of darkness had shined into our hearts to give us the light of the knowledge of the glory of God in the face of Jesus Christ." We can as safely dispense with the work of the Son, as with the work of the Holy Spirit, in the matter of our redemption; and hence it is that the dispensation of the spirit is so distinctly marked and so prominently set forth in the word of God. The annointing oil was an appropriate and beautiful emblem of his sweet and gracious influences. With this, in most solemn and significant formalities, the high priest was annointed, the tabernacle and all the vessels of the ministry. It was poured on Aaron's head, and ran down his beard, and flowed even to the skirts of his garments. From these authenticated shadows of heavenly things, we turn our favored eyes to the heavenly things themselves; to our great High Priest, as he stands on the banks of the Jordan, where the shadow is lost in the substance, where the spirit descends in form like a dove and rests upon him. And from him, the great Head of the Church, it flows to all the members of his mystic body. It is the oil of gladness, and wins the reluctant heart to cheerful obedience. It is the unction from the Holy One, and the same annointing teacheth the ignorant and them that err from the way, the wisdom and the way of the just. Jesus came to obey and to die in the room of his people. It was not in the economy of redemption, committed to him personally to furnish the New Testament Scriptures, or to gather the New Testament Church. By him not a single line was written, not a single church was formed. These events followed his ascension, and he assured his disciples that they were, by previous arrangement, and according to the determinate council of God, to occur in this order and manner; that when he had finished the work given him to do on earth, the glorious economy must be arrested forever at that point, and never be issued and completed, except he should ascend up where he was before, and prepare the way for another comforter, who was the Holy Ghost, and whose designated work could be accomplished by no other. "It is expedient for you that I go away; for if I go not away the comforter will not come unto you. And when he is come he will reprove the world of sin and of righteousness and of judgment. Of sin, because they believe not in me; of righteousness, because I go to my father, and ye see me no more; of judgment, because the prince of this world is judged. John xvi. 7, 11. No preaching was to be attempted, no Scripture written, no churches gathered. " Tarry ye in the city of Jerusalem [was the direction,] until ye be endued with power from on high." "And when the day of Pentecost was fully come, they were all with one accord in one place. And suddenly there came a sound from heaven as of a rushing mighty wind, and it filled all the house where they were sitting; and there appeared unto them cloven tongues as of fire, and it sat upon each of them, and they were all filled with the Holy Ghost, and began to speak with other tongues as the spirit gave them utterance." Thus "this Jesus," * * "being by the right hand of God exalted, and having received of the Father the promise of the Holy Spirit, he [said Peter] hath shed forth this which ye now see and hear." And from this blessed hour, God the Holy Ghost, writes out the Scripture canon by his inspiration,—gives the Apostles a mouth and wisdom which none of their adversaries were able to gainsay or resist, and, by an instrumentality denominated the weakness of God and the foolishness of preaching, an instrumentality totally inert in itself, and wholly inadequate to the production of the wonderful result, gathers the church out of the ruins of the fall, and builds it on the "foundations of the apostles and prophets, Jesus Christ himself being the chief corner stone."

The advent of the Son, was not more distinctly marked than was the advent of the Holy Ghost. The Son came and then ascended up where he was before. The Spirit came not to finish the short work of a miraculous testimony and then to depart, but to abide in the church forever, to enlighten the darkened understanding in the things of Christ, to renew the heart and to sanctify the moral nature of man. The union of the human and divine natures in one person forever gave to the atonement its value. But the Holy Spirit proceeding from the Father and the Son, inhabited the human nature also, and filled the human soul with gracious affections, and powerfully acted and infallibly guided that nature in all its ways. If the Son was possessed of a human body and soul, it was created by the Holy Ghost; if led up into the wilderness to be tempted of the devil, it was by the Spirit ; if he returned into Galilee, it was in the power of the Spirit ; if he cast out devils, it was by the Holy Ghost ; if he groaned and was troubled at the grave of Lazarus, it was in the Spirit ; if he preached the gospel and spake as never man spake, it was because the Spirit of the Lord God was upon him, because the Lord had annointed him to preach glad tidings to the meek ; if he, after his resurrection gave commandment unto the apostles, whom he had chosen, it was by the Holy Ghost ; in fine, as his entire humiliation was vicarious, so every part of it partook wholly and only of that character, he did nothing *of* himself, or *for* himself, but by the Holy Ghost and for his people. Our Lord had wisdom and power and every excellence in an infinite degree as the Son of God, coequal and coeternal with the Father, and could have instructed and commanded the disciples in all wisdom and righteousness without the Spirit, but for the peculiar economy under which he acted. This rendered the intervention of the Holy Ghost necessary. The first man Adam was a living soul, and rendered obedience in his own strength. When he fell, the second man Adam took his place, with the intention of restoring to him, and to vast multitudes of his posterity their lost righteousness and ability, and as the former was to be imputed, and the latter imparted, his whole work must be regarded as vicarious, and all his endowments as new, peculiar, and as bearing directly on the grand result. He was filled with the Holy Ghost for our sakes, that he might create a spiritual kingdom, to rest upon a mediatorial basis, to be sustained by the Son, and be beautified by the spirit forever. Every other department of God's moral kingdom rests upon a natural basis, and is happy or miserable according as is the natural character of moral beings, contained within its limits, good or bad. But it is not so with Messiah's kingdom and reign in this the righteousness is not natural, but external to the subject, and becomes his, only in the judgment of God, and here also the strength and holiness of the subject is not natural, but spiritual and imparted by the Holy Ghost. If then, the Son of God wrought all his miracles, not by that power which was natural to him, but by the Holy Ghost, and loved, obeyed, and suffered, and rose again by the power of the same spirit, and after his resurrection gave commandments to the apostles whom he had chosen by the Holy Ghost, and after his ascension continued to order and to establish, gather, and edify his glorious kingdom by the same blessed agent, then how can men, mere men, fallen and sinful men, expect to render acceptable obedience in their own strength, or indeed any spiritual obedience whatever, without the spirit? never was there an opinion more unscriptural, never was there an expectation more fallacious. The doctrine of natural ability is at war with every feature in the covenant of grace, with the whole economy of redemption. The obedience which we are able to render of ourselves, is merely natural; that which God requires under the new covenant is purely spiritual, and as many as are led by the Spirit of God, these are the Sons of God, and are built on the foundation of the Apostles and Prophets, Jesus Christ himself being the chief corner stone, in whom all the building fitly framed together groweth up into an holy temple in the Lord. The Church is called spiritual, because the human nature of her Lord was created by the Spirit, inhabited by the Spirit, and quickened by the Spirit; when he ascended he shed forth the Spirit on the church to make a miraculous testimony, to finish the record concerning God's dear Son, to renew and sanctify the saints; and thus the whole church is placed under the ministration of the spirit, is born of the spirit, enlightened by the spirit, quickened by the spirit, led by the spirit, sanctified by the spirit, and is become the habitation of God through the spirit, and God hath made us able ministers of the New Testament, not of the letter, but of the spirit. for the letter killeth, but the spirit giveth life." 2 Cor. iii. 6.

There is a just and obvious distinction between a natural and a gracious ability. The former is that which we possess in common with all animated nature. "In him we live and move and have our being." The latter is an ability flowing from the Holy Spirit, whereby we are raised from our death in sin, and disposed and enabled to render evangelical obedience. By the former we are enabled to attend to all the duties of a natural religion. By the latter we are enabled to attend to all the duties of a supernatural religion. Mere nature cannot originate anything different from itself; in all its changes it remains what it was; flesh is flesh; the stream never rises above its fountain. The Jews employed natural ability and it produced religion in abundance, but it was like its origin, it was not spiritual, but natural. The law of moral necessity which binds a sinful moral nature to its perpetual identity is as mighty as that which binds the planets in their revolutions and motions; it never can be resisted or overcome by anything contained within itself. If this is not true, (as the New School affirm that it is not,) if fallen man is as able to do that which is spiritually good as he is to "arise and walk," or as he is to perform any other natural actions, then there can be no necessity for the spirit's supernatural work, and all the probabilities are against the existence of such a work. If the present universe could have rolled itself from the bosom of a primeval chaos, and by its own laws of chemical action, could have covered itself with verdure, and beauty, and life, then the account of Moses is at once discredited, for he assigns for its existence a supernatural cause, when one merely natural was sufficient. And in like manner, if fallen man has an ability appropriately his own, and sufficient to all the ends of a spiritual obedience, no other ability can reasonably be prayed for, or expected. That which can create itself, furnishes by its existence no evidence or display of divine wisdom, or Omnipotence. If the new heavens and the new earth, wherein dwelleth righteousness, are but Jewish allegories and could create themselves, then the wonderful agency of the Holy Ghost was not demanded, either to originate or to garnish them. There must be a necessity for the work of the spirit immutably fixed in the very nature of the things to be done, or else no such work is to be expected from him. To declare the contrary, to deny this necessity for the spirit's influence, is, as to all ultimate purposes, a denial of its existence and exercise. It is a truth, which lodges itself in the mind by irresistable deduction, that God never puts forth his power in the performance of any work which could as well succeed without him. That would be a folly which infinite wisdom could not enact; a display of power unbecoming himself, and without a parallel in the works of his hands. The author of the vestiges of creation, by maintaining that the universe assumed its present form and filled itself with beauty and life, by the concurrence of accidental chemical affinities, has indirectly maintained that God did not create the world according to the Mosaic account : because the power of God was not required to do what nature could do without it, and hence, the inference is irresistable that God did not create the universe. For if the extravagant hypothesis be once admitted, that matter had a natural ability to take the shape of worlds, and to engender animal and vegetable life upon their surfaces, then as no other power was necessary, so no other power was exercised. As the phenomena can be explained on natural principles, it is absurd to go beyond them into that which is supernatural for an explanation.— Hence if God has given to man a natural ability to obey without the Holy Spirit, then that is sufficient, then anything farther would be uncalled for and absurd, then the spirit is not given, and there can be no assignable reason why he should be given.

The ability of man to "repent and believe to the saving of his soul" without the aid of the Holy Spirit, is precisely the same, according to Mr. Duffield, with his ability to arise and walk" without the aid of the Holy Spirit. And as the Holy Spirit is not given to aid men to "arise and walk" for the plain reason that they are already able to perform these natural actions, so for the same reasons we must conclude he is not given to aid us to repent and believe. We cannot accordingly be dependent on his agency for repentance, faith or regeneration, and it would be absurd either to pray for it, or expect it. Would the man in good health, who had the fear of God before his eyes, dare to pray for the special descent of the Holy Spirit to enable him to "arise and walk?" God has given him power already to perform these motions, and man would be guilty of profaneness, were he to pray that God would additional to this, send down from heaven the third person of the blessed Trinity, in a special and distinct ministration, to enable him to "arise and walk." And if saving repentance and faith are equally within our power, then to pray for the Spirit's aid in their origin or exercise would be profanity, and an expectation of his presence madness. These conclusions are irresistable; they force themselves upon us, and lead us to tremble for the safety of those who crowd the vestibule that leads to them. They shroud the future with a night, whose terriffic gloom it requires more than ordinary daring and hardness to encounter; and ah, what shall be the end of those who are captivated and led astray by them? Many are already quite fallen—lost in skepticism and infidelity, they sport with their own deceivings, and their steps take hold on hell. That course of instruction which throws man back upon his own resources, takes him off in the same degree from all dependence on those which are spiritual and divine. He may be thankful for his ability, but he will not be very likely to pray for help while he remains conscious that he can help himself. The practical issues of this belief are invariably the same; prayer is abandoned. The cry to heaven for help breaks from the deck of the ship when the ship itself is broken by the waves. In that dark hour of peril and despair, when one cannot help another and no one can help himself, even heathens cast their final hope on the everlasting arm. "Arise! Call upon thy God, if so be that God will think upon us that we perish not." Jonah i. 6. Sincere and earnest prayer for help comes from the helpless, not from those who can help themselves.

The denial of the doctrine of native depravity also invades and vacates the work of the Holy Ghost, by denying the existence of the very thing to be removed by his blessed agency. For what can be more obvious than that if there is no natural depravity in existence, then there can be no call for the Spirit's agency to remove it. The war made upon native depravity, is the indirect war upon the Spirit's necessity. If native depravity be mere theory, mere philosophy, a mere figment, then the Spirit's agency in removing it, is mere theory, mere philosophy, a mere figment. The hand therefore, that wipes out the deep polluting imprint of the fall from the cheek of nature, is extended in the same act to blot out the record and the glory and the work of the Spirit's ministration. For if there is no natural depravity in the soul or any of its faculties, if men can understand the truth as it is in Jesus, and choose and love God, of themselves and without the aid of the Holy Ghost, if there are no native defects to be removed by the Spirit, to enable man to obey God, then it is not true that "He opens the understanding that we should understand the Scriptures," (Luke xxiv. 45) renews the will and heart that we should love God; for a good argument, a strong motive is all that can be required to these ends.

When Peter preached the Gospel to the Gentiles, it was according to this view, not the "Holy Ghost which fell on them that heard the word," (Acts x. 44) but the inspired argument of Peter, which effected their conversion. And when Lydia heard the word, it was not required that the

"Lord should open her heart to receive the things spoken by Paul," (Acts xvi. 14) as the things spoken were sufficient of themselves to sway her mind and change her governing purpose, without any direct action upon her heart by the Holy Ghost. And this is the precise alternative to which the New School resort. Regeneration is to be by moral suasion.— This Dr. Duffield attempts through several pages to prove, and Mr. Gilbert, the permanent clerk of the New School General Assembly in 1838, published a pamphlet by request of his brethren in the ministry, entitled "Moral Suasion," or "Regeneration no miracle."

Whatever may be said by these men concerning the necessity and power of the Spirit in regeneration, so long as the Spirit is nevertheless, carefully and fully excluded from the performance of any direct work on the heart itself, in imparting to it any new principle of spiritual life, it is all the same as though they had said nothing concerning the Spirit at all ; for if his power is arrested by the argument and expends itself upon it, and does not touch the guilty soul by a direct and creative energy and impart to it spiritual life, then regeneration is the act of the sinner, and not the act of God. Let the infinite motives, if you please, be drawn from three worlds, and pressed, it matters not how, or by whom, since this is all, for if the sinner's heart is changed by the presentation of motives, then he changes it himself. He who is induced to change his mind by a strong persuasion, still does the act himself. It is appropriately his act, and cannot be said in that case to be the act of any other. But this is not regeneration at all. The entire doctrine is abandoned and rejected by such a definition of it. Regeneration is an inward spiritual and supernatural work of the Holy Ghost, impossible to be done by man. It is in no respect the act of man, but in every respect the act of God. The sinner does not beget himself but, is begotten of God. He is wholly passive in regeneration. He does not in it perform but receives an action, as when the woman was healed by the virtue that went out of our blessed Lord, though active in touching his garment, yet the act of healing was his, not hers. She was wholly passive with respect to that act.—Neither was it by any words spoken by the Redeemer, but by a virtue that went out of him that she was healed. (Mark v. 30.) Thus, in regeneration, though active in the use of means, though putting forth every effort that we may but touch the hem of his garments and draw virtue out of him, yet the life which we receive is from him. It is not self-originated, but divinely imparted. This is too plain to be misunderstood, too conclusive to be evaded. It is usual, however, to object that the mind is not an agent that acts or that receives an action in a state of passivity, but is in itself essentially active, and therefore active in regeneration. It will not be necessary to a successful defence of our position, to discuss this new theory concerning the nature of the mind. We have only to say that there is a just and natural distinction between life and the motions of life. Though these may not be distinguishable in the order of time, yet they are in the order of nature. Say, then, that the activities of the sinner as a moral being are not for an *instant* suspended, either before or after regeneration, that even at the very moment of it, his whole soul was roused into a state of most intense activity, yet this cannot affect the question of his passivity with respect to the acts of an agent wholly extraneous to himself. Those acts are not his, he does not perform them, and hence when the Holy Spirit imparts to him a new kind of life, a life which he never had and could not originate in himself, imparts it at once, and diffuses it through all his soul, he receives an action from without himself, and that action is in no respect his own. When the new life is given, he of course puts forth its motions; the motions of the new life are his, but the life itself is communicated. So that whatever view we may take of the mind, of its successive states or essential activities, it is all the same with respect to the question at issue: and we therefore repeat the charge, that the entire doctrine of regeneration is abandoned and rejected by the New School definition of it : I speak not of professions, but of facts. They retain the word but destroy its meaning, turn it into an apple of Sodom, fair without but within full of cinders and ashes, give us pewter for silver, and brass for gold, pervert and darken a plain question, and then ask us if we cannot see clearly that the whole dispute "is not about a fact, but about the mere philosophy of a fact?" Not whether we are regenerated, but *how* we are regenerated? when at the same time the dispute is about the great fact of regeneration itself, whether indeed spiritual life is imparted to the soul, or whether it is not. Whether indeed, any principles are imparted by the Holy Ghost, new, spiritual and supernatural, wholly unlike any thing we ever had before, and which we could not originate in ourselves, or whether this old doctrine of the Church and of the Bible is the relic of a dark age. For, whether motives are or are not presented to sinners in the gospel call, is not a question in controversy, and it never has been. We all believe they are, and it is a mere evasion to talk about them in the discussion of a totally distinct matter. But is regeneration the act of God the Spirit, does he perform it upon us, does he "take away the stony heart out of our flesh and give us a heart of flesh," (Eze. xxxvi. 26) are we born of the Spirit, "not of blood, not of the will of the flesh, nor of the will of man, but of God?" (John i. 13.) In a word, is the new heart "created" (Eph. ii. 10) by the Holy Spirit, or is there no such act of creative omnipotence required or exercised? The question is as to this fact: and if it does not exist, as our opponents maintain it does not, then there is no such thing as regeneration as understood by the Church, and the New School are convicted of denying the doctrine altogether.

They in effect make truth an agent; this is the necessary

result of their philosophy. "The power which God exerts in the conversion of a soul, is moral power; it is that kind of power by which a statesman sways the mind of a senate, or by which an advocate moves and bows the heart of a jury." (Finney's sermons on important subjects, pp. 21, 27, 28, 30.) "Shall we suppose that God cannot do with sinners, in reference to himself, what one man has done with another; that a physical efficiency is necessary to make the sinner willing to confide in him. * * "It would be, in effect, to say that man can subdue his foe, and, by an appropriate moral influence, convert him into a friend, but that God cannot convert his enemy, and bring him to believe, except he puts forth his physical power, and literally creates him over again." (Duffield on Regeneration, pp. 492, 493.) I find Mr. Barnes referring in different places of his Commentary to his Notes on 2 Cor. v. 14. "If any man be in Christ, he is a new creature: old things are passed away; behold, all things are become new." And here I find the following statements: "The mode or manner in which it is done, is not described, nor should the words be pressed to the quick, as if the process were the same in both cases;" (i. e.) "a change, so to speak, as if the man were made over again." * * "If a drunkard becomes reformed, there is no impropriety in saying that he is a new man." * * "There is such a change as to make the language proper, and so in the conversion of a sinner." And in Rom. v. 19, he teaches that man is plunged in sin by the first Adam, in the same way that the families of drunkards and pirates are ruined; by a social organization. "And by the same organization he shall, through the second Adam rise to life, and ascend to the skies," i. e., by gospel truth and christian example; for in Rom. iv. 3, he further explains himself: "Faith is always an act of the mind; it is not a principle, * * * "God promises, man believes, and this is the whole of it." Faith, then, according to Mr. Barnes, is no principle of living union to Christ. Nothing imparted to the soul by the Holy Ghost, but simply an act exercised in view of a motive. The New School, therefore however unwilling they may be to admit it, make the truth an agent, and invest it with a delegated omnipotence. They take the Spirit's work and glory from him, and give it over to eloquent harangues and mighty appeals. Their error is a reproduction of *reason* in her triumphal car, and surrounded by her worshippers; there is a pretender on the throne, an usurper of the prerogatives of God.

The gospel is not an efficient cause; it is "the weakness of God" and "the foolishness of preaching." It has no power in itself, or by communication to it, to raise the dead in sin; and because of its innate and necessary weakness in the matter of our regeneration, it is the chosen emblem of the power of God, who employs it. It is full of persuasions, but they are poured upon the ears of dead men; the excellency of the power resides in God; (2 Cor. iv. 9;) and at every step in the progress of expostulation and appeal, the admonition should reach our ears and affect our hearts. "It is not by might, or by power, but by my spirit, saith the Lord.' Ezek. iv. 6. "The gospel to the believer is not in word only, but also in power, and in the Holy Ghost, and in much assurance." The power is in the Holy Ghost, and he does not delegate it to words and sentences. He exercises it himself, and does not give his glory to another, nor his praise to motives. He teaches us "what is the exceeding greatness of his power to us-ward, who believe according to the working of his mighty power, which he wrought in Christ, when he raised him from the dead, and set him at his own right hand in heavenly places." Eph. i. 19, 20. The resurrection of the body of Christ from the tomb of Joseph, was a wonderful event, and the effect of a direct act of omnipotence. It was not words; It was the spirit, which created that blessed body at the first, out of nothing, which now quickened its mangled and mortal remains. If words are uttered when the dead are raised, they have no efficiency, but serve to warn us of the outgoings of omnipotence, in its direct and reproductive energy; the power flows out of the spirit—not out of his words. In the same record in which we are told that God said, "Let the waters under the heaven's be gathered into one place." (Gen. i. 9.) It is also stated that "the spirit of God moved upon the face of the waters." (Gen. i. 2.) The word spoken was not an efficient cause ; it did not move on the face of the waters, nor gather them together in one place. The sentence "Lazarus come forth." (John. xi. 43 ;) indicated the will of Christ, but in itself it had no power, as it echoed through the dreary vault, to startle the ear sealed up by the finger of death; the power was not communicated to the words, but to the body of Lazarus, and hence he obeyed the summons of his maker. There could be no power in the sentence itself, nor in the frequency of its repetition ; if ever since the moment it fell from the lips of our blessed Lord, it had continued to be repeated by him, unaccompanied by his divine power directly acting on the body, the sleep of Lazarus would never have been broken. Nor could it reside in its loudness ; a thousand parks of artillery discharged over him could not have waked the dead ; earth's internal fires might have been kindled, and rolled their mightiest thunders underneath his resting place of quaking marble, and rocked the surrounding mountains in their beds, but Lazarus would have still continued to sleep on, in the total unconciousness of death. And in like manner, the gospel, is in itself powerless, and holds the same relation to the resurrection of the soul, dead in sin, that it or any other words would, to the resurrection of a body mouldering in the grave. The power, the creative and subjective power, is the same in both cases. Life is life, whether spiritual, or natural, and the one, is as difficult to originate as the other. As it is written the resurrection to spiritual life, is " according to the working of the mighty power of God," (Eph. i. 19.) in the resurrection of our murdered Lord, from the dead. The power, we therefore conclude, resides not in the gospel : neither in its nature nor by communication to it. "It is the spirit that quickeneth," (it is) by my spirit saith the Lord." He is the agent, the great agent, and the only agent, in the act of regeneration ; we are "born of the Spirit."

When Peter, I insist therefore, preached the gospel in the call of the Gentiles, it was not the word that fell on them, that brought them to Christ ; but it is stated that the Holy Ghost fell on them which heard the word." It was not the Scriptures which opened the understanding of the disciples, but it is written, "then opened he their understandings, that they should understand the Scriptures." The things spoken by Paul did not open the heart of Lydia to attend to the gospel call, but the "Lord opened her heart." In all these instances truth is powerless, and the gospel the "weakness of God." It has no sweet voice to "charm the deaf adder." (Ps. iii. 3, 5.) No motives to sway "an iron sinew." (Isai. xlviii. 4.) No eloquent appeal to melt " an adamant stone." (Zech. vii. 12.) Its tears fall upon a rock, its call is lost upon the wind, except the Holy Ghost, first, give the ear to hear and the heart to understand. Isai. xlviii. 8. Native depravity then exists as a melancholy fact and human impotence as a humbling reality. These sad results of Adams fall, are no mere chimeras of the brain, no imaginary streams whose fountains were never opened, and whose waters never flowed, they prevail every where, and all the high hills which are under the whole heaven are covered. No mere words can gather them back again to their beds and restore life to the bosom of a perished world ; the spirit of God must first "move upon the face of the waters."

While the means of grace are not to be made to occupy the place and perform the work of the spirit, they are still neither to be dispised nor neglected, for they are inseparably connected with the end by divine appointment. The prophet in the valley of vision, did not neglect to call upon the dead to live, though their bones were dry and marrowless, and though they had for ages, encumbered the field of the slain. And by this striking and well known example, we are taught to use the means, not because they are efficient, but because they are appointed, and to expect in the diligent use of them, the glorious outgoings of divine power, in the resurrection of the " whole house of Israel." Ez. xxxvii. 1, 14.

Fire is a natural cause, efficient from its own properties, to destroy combustible materials. Its action on them is uniform; whatever will burn when thrown into it, it invariably consumes. The Gospel is no such cause; it does not act uniformly, nor from its essential properties. Peter preached it, and three thousand were brought to repentance: Stephen preached it to men of like passions, with equal sweetness and fidelity, but his exasperated hearers stoned him to death.— " It is the Spirit that quickeneth, the flesh profiteth nothing."

The gospel is not a moral law but a gracious remedy, and assumes as it comes forth from the presence-chamber of the great King, that the world is a lost world, a spiritual charnal-house, in which sin has gathered and piled the whitened bones of ruined generations. It comes to break the strength of sin, and to terminate the reign of death; its voice is that of the Son of God, " the dead hear it, and they that hear live." (John v. 25.) It assumes that sin is an incurable disease, extending its dreadful ravages to the whole race, and spreading from joint to joint and limb to limb; no soul escapes, and no member of the body; " the whole head is sick and the whole heart is faint;" and from the bosom of suffering huumanity the inquiry is wafted on every breeze, "Is there no balm in Gilead, is there no kind physician there?" And when "there is no eye to pity and no arm to save," no voice to break the fearful silence, the Gospel comes, swift as the roe, or the young hart, on the mountains of Bether, bearing an invaluable remedy, and proclaiming a balm for every wound, and a physician who never lost a patient.

In this manner the Gospel every where assumes the helpless, hopeless ruin of the whole world. The dead are already perished; the sick are already past all cure, except by miracle. Whoever, then, falsifies or weakens this assumption, operates in the same way on the remedy itself: it brings it into disrepute; "the whole need not a physician, but they that are sick." (Math. x. 12.) On the contrary, whatever tends to increase the knowledge and conviction of its truth, tends, in the same degree, to bring the great remedy into demand. Hence the prophets and apostles were every where full in their instructions on this point. They asserted its truth, assumed it on all occasions, and illustrated it in every possible way. According to them, the sinner's bones are dry, his disease incurable, his eyes are blind, his feet are lame, his strength is weakness, his wisdom folly, his righteousness filthy rags, the imagination of every thought is evil, he is altogether become unprofitable, his ear is the deaf adder's, his mind and conscience defiled, his heart an adamant stone. This is the uniform image of ruin, and the dark picture is no where relieved, no where softened, with a lighter shade, by the inspired writers. And when the Spirit operates on the sinner's heart, his first work is in perfect correspondence with this, his testimony. The secure sinner, whose heart is touched by the Spirit, finds himself *lost*—the pit into which his convictions plunge him, is the horrible sepulcher of his righteousness and strength: both are decayed at once, and God alone can help him in his need. He, therefore, who denies this truth, belies this Bible testimony, and the Spirit's convictions, and veils the remedy from the eyes of ruined men. I know of no one thing, more contrary to all the instructions of the word of God, or more highly calculated to do an awakened sinner infinite harm, than this fatal error. The assurance of strength in ourselves, is invariably accompanied by the feeling of security. If that feeling of security is taken from us, and our ruin is seen and felt to be complete and appalling, in every aspect of it, then alone we betake ourselves to the cross with a loud and bitter cry: restore it again, and we become secure in sin. There is death, in this error on depravity; it stupifies and destroys the soul; it heals the hurt of the daughter of my people slightly, and leaves the disease to work our final ruin at its leisure. I warn you, therefore, against it. You need to know the nature, and extent of your ruin, rather than that it should be hid from your eyes by flattering words. If you would ever avail yourselves of the remedy, your necessity must be felt; for if you are not dead, you cannot be brought to life, not lost, you cannot be found, not born in sin, you cannot be born again. The physician heals no one who can heal himself; no one shall glory in his presence. As total depravity is a reality, so the conviction of our guilt and impotence must be real and conclusive, and the praise unhesitating; "Unto him that loved us and washed us from our sins in his own blood, and made us kings and priests unto God, and his Father, unto him be glory and dominion forever." No tongue shall falter in that song in heaven, or fear to ascribe too much of the great work to the Son and Spirit, and too little to themselves. Grace began, and continued, and completed, the entire redemption, and faith places the Lamb in the midst of the throne, and crowns are cast down and dominions bow in adoring wonder there. No one is there, who does not wear the bridegroom's robe, "the clean white linen, which is the righteousness of the saints." No one is there, who could or did redeem himself, or who could, or did prepare himself thereunto. In that vast assembly of ransomed sinners, the recollections of past guilt and impotence are the same in all. There is no dust of human ability or righteousness in the balances of that sanctuary; the "righteousness and strength of all are in the Lamb alone." (Isaiah xlv. 24.) In the ascriptions of that song, "Worthy is the Lamb, for he was slain, and hath redeemed us to God by his blood, out of every kindred and tongue and people and nation," the voices are many, but united, the harmony perfect, the melody subduing, the sound vast and comprehensive as that of many waters. There are none round about the throne among all the host of the redeemed, who cannot now unite in ascribing all to grace. And there shall in no wise appear there, hereafter, any thing whatsoever that worketh abomination, or that loveth or that maketh a lie against this truth. He that does not partake of the ruin cannot partake of the remedy, nor join in the praises of the deliverer who said, "I came not to call the righteous but sinners to repentance;" "the whole need not a physician, but the sick."

The New School then deny the necessity of the work of the Holy Spirit in regeneration and make that work improbable and superfluous by asserting the natural ability of man, without the spirit's aid, to do in and for himself, all that God requires in his word. They render his work also an impossibility, by denying that death in sin, or that natural depravity, which alone calls for the spirits supernatural agency. He cannot quicken a soul dead in sin, when no such death in sin exists. He cannot remove a depravity of nature, when there is no such depravity to remove. And finally by their doctrine of moral suasion, they take the spirit's work and glory from him and give them to another. They treat the Holy Spirit as the Papists do the Son; they occupy his place with a strange God Rome has done it with a wafer; they have done it with a motive. These splendid discoveries have called forth the praises of Unitarians, but have filled the church of Christ with strife and alienations. " And the third angel sounded, and there fell a great star from heaven, burning as it were a lamp, and it fell upon the third part of the rivers, and upon the fountains of waters; and the name of the star is called wormwood: and the third part of the waters became wormwood; and many men died of the waters, because they were made bitter." Rev. viii. 10, 11. There is another aspect to this subject which I desire distinctly to bring before your minds. It teaches the annihilation of infants: first, it denies that infants have any moral character, and as our Lord Jesus was an infant once, he is distinctly included. " Things inanimate, have, in Scripture parlance, sometimes been called holy, as the inmost chamber of the temple was called the Holy of Holies. But then it was because of some especial and peculiar relationship, it had to God. He dwelt in it; it was set apart as preeminently and exclusively appropriated to God. In this sense, the yet unconscious human nature of Christ, may be denominated holy, for it was the habitation of God, and singularly and exclusively appropriated to him, differing, in this respect, essentially and entirely from that of any of the descendants of Adam." "It is obvious, that in infancy and incipient childhood, when none of the actions are deliberate, or the result of motive operating in connection with the knowledge of the law and of the great end of all human actions, no moral character can properly be predicated;" "properly speaking, therefore, we can predicate of it, neither sin nor holiness, personally considered," (see Duffield on Regeneration,pp. 377, 378, 379, 353.) From the above extracts, among other things, we are taught that the human nature of Christ was once holy in the same sense in which the most holy place was holy, not really, but relatively, or in the same sense in which a linen curtain or a board is holy, (i. e.) was not holy at all. But the Scriptures teach that Jesus was created and born holy; " the Holy Ghost shall come upon thee, and the power of the Highest shall overshadow thee, therefore also that holy thing which shall be born of thee, shall be called the Son of God." (Luke i. 13.) To deny that this nature was holy in reality, contradicts the above text, and takes away the principal glory of the nature itself, and the principal glory of the Spirit, in its creation. The views of Mr. Duffield, in common with the New School, on native depravity, lead irresistably to this conclusion, to wit: that the human nature of the infant Jesus was not at first holy, a conclusion not only obviously erroneous, but wanting in every feature of propriety and religious veneration.

And again, if infants have no moral character, they can have no moral nature, for these are inseparable from each other, and then, by necessary consequence, they are in no respect moral beings, and are not the subjects of the moral government of God; they die by the same law by which a brute dies, and perish as the brutes perish. "Animals are not subjects of the moral government of God, neither are infants, previous to moral agency, for what has moral government to do with those who are not moral agents: animals and infants, previous to moral agency, do therefore stand on precisely the same ground in reference to this subject." (See Christian Spectator for 1829, p. 173.) The above reasoning is conclusive, if the premises are admitted, to wit: that intelligent preferences to good and evil are essential to the existence of moral character; for if they are, then they are equally so to the existence of a moral nature, for a moral nature cannot be separated from its character, just as a rainbow cannot be separated from its colors; and hence infants, previous to moral agency, are mere animals. Mr. Barnes evidently holds, with the others of this School, that infants are not "moral agents" as soon as they are born, but that they become such at some subsequent period. (See his 9th *remark* on Rom. v. 19.) Against this doctrine we urge the following objections.

First, it denies our Lord's testimony; "of such [is his emphatic language,] of such is the kingdom of God," (Mark x. 14: and verse 16,) "and he took them up in his arms, put his hands upon them and blessed them." This kingdom of God, of which they are so solemnly recognized as members, is a kingdom of "righteousness and peace and joy in the Holy

Ghost;" (Rom. xiv. 19.) and none can belong to it who are mere animals—mere animals are not redeemed sinners. And as millions of our race pass the gateway into the other world in infancy, and as mere animals, their nature and their end must be the same with all other animals, they must be annihilated; and this falsifies the solemn statement of our Lord, when he said they belonged to the kingdom of God, and turns into absurdity his solemn benediction, when he laid his hands on them and blessed them. It robs him of his reward. He shed his blood for sinners, not for mere animals, and as infants are not sinners, they cannot be washed from their sins in a Saviour's blood, they can have no part nor lot in that matter. It robs the Spirit of his glory, in renewing the natures of infants, for they cannot be renewed by the Holy Ghost: "the washing of regeneration" is applied only to a defiled moral nature, and as there is no such defilement, it cannot be washed away—no such moral nature, previous to moral agency, it cannot be made the subject of renewing influences.

It denies the Abrahamic covenant, and falsifies the significance of both its seals. At the age of eight days the seal of circumcision was applied to the decendents of Abraham, and baptism is authorized at an equally early period. In this solemn transaction, children are recognized as moral beings, possessed of a moral nature, and as sustaining moral relations which reach to the fall of Adam, to the redemption by Christ, and to the sanctification by the Spirit. Such relations belong not to the brute creation, and therefore they are never brought within the provisions of the everlasting covenant, nor profanely baptized in the name of the Father, and the Son, and the Holy Ghost. Over them no gracious conveyances are suspended in the promises, and no prayers are offered to bring them down. In relation to mere animals, such ceremonies would be an abomination, and the consciousness of this fact, has occasioned a growing neglect of infant baptism among the New School. Their apathy has not found formal utterance, but it is the result of their views; for how can they but question the propriety of baptizing, in the name of the Trinity, a mere animal, which may be annihilated in an hour, or praying for the justification and sanctification of a nature wholly free from sin?

This doctrine is odious. Those who first openly avowed it, have found that it would not be borne, and have blenched from the withering gaze of an insulted church. Some however, still privately assert their belief in it, and others yet meet us with the evasions noticed by Dr. Spring in 1833. " They were not prepared either to affirm or deny; but their minds seemed to be in a painful state of hesitation and skepticism. *They could not tell;* they did not know what the Bible taught in relation to the native character of our fallen race. Ask them whether we were born sinners, and they will tell you; *We do not know.* Ask them whether infants possess any moral character, and they would relpy; *we do not know.* Ask them whether they are accountable beings; and they would tell you; *we do not know.* Ask them whether they need the washing of regeneration and the renewing of the Holy Ghost; and they answered; *we do not know.* Ask them what becomes of infants when they die; and they said, *we do not know.* Ask them whether death in relation to infants is by sin; and they still say, *we do not know.*" (See Dissertation on Native Depravity, by Gardner Spring, D. D. pp. 3, 4.) By others again it is suggested that though incapable of regeneration here, yet when they are in heaven, and old enough to choose God, they do so in the first moral and voluntary act. But this places infants in heaven without their ever having sinned, and independently of the work of the Son and Spirit, either in atoning for their sin, or in cleansing them from it, and brings against the whole theory the original objections in all their force, with additional ones, equally formidable, which doom this error of the schools, this offspring of a false philosophy, to its own place. This doctrine, has no consoling words for those "Rachel's who weep for their children, and refuse to be comforted because they are not;" it assures them that they shall never meet them more. No attractions for those parents who with cheerful gratitude and believing hearts, have dedicated their infant offspring to God in baptism, for it assures them that the link which unites their children to the common nature of the domesticated cat and dog, is yet to be broken. Nor can it either find favor with the unsofisticated ministers of Jesus; it teaches them that that child was an animal for which they prayed at its baptism. They prayed that it might now be washed in the blood of atonement, when it had no sin to wash away; they prayed that it might now be renewed by the Holy Ghost, when it had no moral nature to be renewed, no stain to wipe out, no disease to cure. Indeed an error so uncongenial can find little favor any where, and it would soon cease to be known, except to history, but for its connection with its source, the error on native depravity, out of which it grows and of which its very existence is a sufficient refutation. Of this the New School themselves appear painfully conscious and are hence very unwilling either to admit, or deny any thing on the subject of infant regeneration, and when the charge of believing in their annihilation is fairly established by inference from their premises, or by quotations from the open avowels, of some of their less wary champions, they shrink instinctively from the spectre which their wretched philosophy has conjured up, and has placed before their theological chair.

CHAPTER VII.

DOCTRINAL DIFFERENCES CONTINUED.

Revivals of Religion—Views of the Old School on this subject—Differences respecting their nature and genuineness.

An impression prevails that Presbyterians of the Old School, do not believe in revivals of religion, but this is erroneous. The differences between them and the New School are not as to the fact of revivals, but as to the evidences of their genuineness. Religion from various causes may decline in the visible church. Her enjoyment of the means of grace may for a season be partially or wholly interrupted; false teachers, and a corrupting example may surround them; very unfavorable changes may occur in their external circumstances, and from various other causes operating simultaneously, and generally, a declension in vital godliness may come to prevail to an alarming and melancholy extent. And when God changes this state of things revives his work, brings again the captivity of his people, restores to them the means of grace and sheds his spirit upon them, it is a revival—life from the dead—a time of refreshing from the presence of the Lord, and Jacob shall rejoice, and Israel shall be glad.

A great decline in true religion prevailed among the Israelites in Egypt. Their religious privileges were taken away, oppression interrupted their public worship, and their Sabbaths were forgotten. A corrupt literature, a false religion, and an abounding immorality, combined to produce a sad assimilation of the slave to his master, and in the abscence of all counteracting influences, vital godliness lost its visibility, and almost its existence. At this time, Moses was raised up to be a deliverer. Yet so blinded were his brethren ; so brutalized by ignorance and oppression they knew not their friend from their foe. Moses was rejected, and for forty years, remained in the wilderness, maturing in piety, wisdom, and experience, to fit him for the great part he was to act in the approaching reformation; and when the time had fully come, he, under the divine direction, entered on his work. God was with him in outward signs, and in inward influences. The people were delivered, grew in knowledge, and in grace, and the young and rising generation, were made the subjects of a glorious work of grace, and were ultimately settled in the land of Canaan, in a state of great prosperity. The solemn profession of their faith at Gilgal, when Joshua rolled away their reproach, and their religious character, as contrasted with that of the Israelites at any other period of their history, furnishes a gratifying evidence of the genuineness of that great change which had been wrought in them by the Holy Ghost, and of which their circumcision at Gilgal, was the solemn and external avowal and symbolical exhibition : that their circumcision was not merely in the flesh, but also in the heart, whose praise was not of men, but of God. This godly generation, however, soon passed away, and were succeeded by others, among whom, the truly spiritual held an increasingly diminished proportion to the increasing numbers of the people. The children did not grow up from generation to generation in the fear of God, but grew up an increase of sinful men, to augment the fierce anger of the Lord against Israel.

After six centuries had passed away, false prophets had begun to make their appearance in great numbers, and ultimately, by corrupting the true religion, and by introducing a false one, they succeeded in producing a great declension in vital godliness. This state of things was held in check, from time to time, by partial revivals. One of these interesting and merciful visitations occurred during the reign of the good king, Hezekiah. (2 Chron. xxx.) The king being divinely influenced established a decree, to make a proclamation from Beersheba even unto Dan, throughout all Israel,' that they should come to the passover unto the Lord God of Israel, at Jerusalem, for they had not done it of a long time in such sort as it was written. So the posts went with the letters from the king and his princes throughout all Israel and Judah, and according to the commandment of the king, saying, "ye children of Israel turn again unto the Lord God of Abraham, Isaac and Israel, and he will return to the remnant of you that are escaped out of the hands of the king of Assyria. And be not ye like your fathers and like your brethren, which trespassed against the Lord God of their fathers, who therefore gave them up to dessolation, as ye see. Now, be ye not stiff-necked as your fathers were, but yield yourselves unto the Lord, and enter into his sanctuary which he hath sanctified forever; and serve the Lord your God, that the fierceness of his wrath may turn away from you. For if ye turn again unto the Lord, your brethren and your children shall find compassion before them that lead them captive, so that they shall come again unto this land, for the Lord your God is gracious and merciful, and will not turn away his face from you if ye return unto him. So the posts passed from city to city, through the country of Ephraim and Manasseh, even unto Zebulon." But so lost were the people to the power of true religion, so blinded had they become in sin, and so hardened in a way that was not good, that they treated the message with contempt, and insulted the messengers. "They laughed them to scorn, and mocked them." This was, however, not universal, for "divers of Asher and Manasseh, and of Zebulon, humbled themselves and came to Jerusalem; also in Judah the hand of God was to give them one heart to do the commandments of the king and of the princes, by the word of the Lord."

The assemblage at Jerusalem was very great, the reformation very thorough. Those who, amid abounding impiety, had neglected too long, their ceremonial cleansing, to be fully prepared, in this respect, for the eating of the passover, were, nevertheless, permitted to partake, because if they had experienced the inward cleansing, the ceremonial could not be of such indispensable moment. And, accordingly, Hezekiah prayed for them, saying, "the good Lord pardon every one that prepareth his *heart* to seek God, the Lord God of his fathers, though he be not cleansed according to the purification of the sanctuary; and the Lord hearkened to Hezekiah and healed the people, and after seven days had been spent in this delightful manner, the congregation found themselves unwilling to separate—they could linger there forever, and they kept other seven days with gladness.— and all the congregation of Judah with the priests and the Levites, and all the congregation that came out of Israel, and the strangers that came out of the land of Israel, and that dwelt in Judah, rejoiced. So there was great joy in Jerusalem, for since the time of Solomon the son of David, King of Israel, there was not the like in Jerusalem. Then the priests and the Levites arose and blessed the people and their voice was heard and their prayer came up to his holy dwelling-place, even unto heaven." This is an inspired record of a glorious revival of true religion. It was promoted by using the means which God had appointed. In the diligent and reverent use of these means the people were blessed with the pardon of their sins, their souls were healed, the whole congregation filled with spiritual joy, and all abounded in the exercise of gracious affections. Such a work of grace had not occurred before in two hundred and eighty-eight years. The divine influences were abundant and refreshing. The time to favor Zion, yea the set time had come.

After this blessed manifestation of God's favor to his

people, true religion again greatly declined, so that at the end of seven hundred years it appeared almost extinct on earth. External washings, the blood of bulls, and of goats, and a strict attention to outward forms, were regarded as of more avail than the sacrifice of a broken and a contrite heart. The Pharisees, especially, were very exact in the observance of numerous rites and ceremonies, both of divine and of human institution. They labored mainly for effect, not on the heart, but on the imagination, through the use of imposing ceremonies, and by the display of an ostentatious wisdom and sanctity. They made broad their phylacteries, and enlarged the borders of their garments, were ever ready to pay tithe of mint, annise, and cummin, but corrupt at heart and entirely neglecting the weightier matters of the law, judgment, and the love of God. The notions of heathen philosophers, together with adulterated theories of their own religion were the husks with which they fed the multitude. Such were the blind guides of the people, such were the characters of the most learned and influential in the visible church. The wretched inhabitants of Judea had imbibed their errors and were bewildered in the valley of the shadow of death, but spiritual blindness was not confined to Judea alone, throughout the vast empire of Rome, and throughout all the earth, the demon of darkness exerted an uncontrolled influence, and his deluded votaries were led captive by him at his will. Philosophers, whose intellectual cultivation and endowments gave them a noble elevation, taught that all crimes were equal; that theft and adultery were lawful; that it was right for parents to roast and eat their children, or for children to roast and eat their parents: yea, inasmuch as they did not like to retain God in their knowledge, they thought that the Godhead was made like unto wood and stone graven by art and man's devise, and from a corrupted religion issued a corrupted moral and social condition. The work of desolation was complete, everything noble in the character of man was prostituted. All around, and in every circle, among the highest as well as the lowest, among Jews as well as Gentiles, the darkness was visible and might be felt. It was at this time, when true piety seemed to have left the earth forever, it was at this time of utter desertion and despair, that the day-spring from on high began to dawn and the sun of righteousness arose above the horizon of the moral heavens. The Redeemer of sinners stood on the earth, and looking around on the benighted nations, rejoiced in the spirit and said, "I am the light of the world, he that followeth me shall not walk in darkness, but shall have the light of life." After the resurrection of Jesus the Apostles were endued with power from on high; evangelical truth spread in every direction; the spirit was shed forth in his quickening influences; an awakened interest, attended and followed the gospel testimony; many thousands were pained on account of their sin, and were led by faith to behold the Lamb of God, who taketh away the sin of the world. But not among the Jews alone, the revival spread also among the Gentiles; "of a truth, cried the astonished Peter, God hath granted unto the Gentiles repentance unto life." It was a favored hour—a time of refreshing from the presence of the Lord, when he was made known unto them that sought him not; and was made manifest unto them that asked not after him. The infinite and hopeless distance between a holy God, and the polluted and degraded Gentile, was at once traversed by the footsteps of bleeding mercy; the long and dreary silence was broken, and the wilderness and the solitary place became glad for them, and the desert did bud and blossom as the rose.

It is true that this was an age of miracles, and, these were to answer their end and pass away, but there were blessings in this age which were not to be transient but permanent. These were the blessings of inward and supernatural grace with which the age abounded. Though the healing of the sick, the raising of the dead, and the gift of tongues were not to be the ordinary and perpetual concomitants of the gospel, yet he who was exalted to convince the whole world of sin, because they believed not on him, by the effusion of his Holy Spirit and to give repentance unto Israel and the forgiveness of sins, was exalted to do it in every age as truly as in the early out-goings of a primitive Christianity. Other sheep, said he, have I, which are not of this fold, them also must I bring, and they *shall* hear my voice. The ministry received a commission to preach the gospel to all men and to all ages even to the end of time. If it can be said in any age, in any place, as it once was, "I have much people in this city," there, a faithful ministry shall preach the gospel, there, men hitherto indifferent, shall become solicitous concerning their salvation, and shall inquire what they shall do to be saved. Gifts of healing in a supernatural way, were not to be continued except as they were connected with the gospel testimony and with the quickening power of the Holy Ghost, on the soul dead in sin. In this respect a constant miracle was to distinguish the blessed gospel and that in all ages. Glorious things are spoken of thee, Oh, thou city of God. It shall be said of this and of that man, they were born in Zion and the highest himself shall establish her.

True revivals, then, result from a divine and supernatural agency ; in Judah, when the memorable passover was celebrated by Hezekiah, the hand of God was to give every one a heart to execute the commandments of the Lord. By Ezekiel it is said, in reference to a glorious event of this kind, "then will I sprinkle clean water upon you, and ye shall be clean from all your filthiness, and from all your idols will I cleanse you; a new heart, also, will I give you, and I will take away the stony heart out of your flesh, and will give you an heart of flesh." When Peter preached the gospel on the day of Pentecost, three thousand were pricked in the heart, and the Lord added to the church daily such as should be saved: according as it is written, and thus it behooves us to acknowledge the Holy Ghost in his official and blessed work, and to say "not by might, or by power, but by my spirit saith the Lord." "To as many as received him, to them gave he power to become the sons of God, even to them that believed on his name, who were born, not of blood, nor of the will of the flesh, nor of the will of man, but of God. When the Gentiles were called, the Holy Ghost fell on them which heard the word.

True revivals occur in connection with means divinely appointed. Hezekiah employed the passover, a divinely appointed festival, to promote a work of grace, and the Apostles went everywhere preaching Jesus, as they were authorised to do, making the Old Testament scriptures the basis of their instructions; the first day of the week, ordinarily the time for communicating their message; baptism, the outward sign of an inward grace, the seal of the covenant, and the pledge of love and fidelity; the Lord's supper, the commemoration of the Lord's death, and the means of comfort and support, the outward and solemn declaration of faith in a Saviour's sacrifice.

When true revivals occur, believers, some of them at least, are greatly quickened and divinely led to seek after them as blessings inexpressably great and desirable. Moses never lost sight of the great end which he sought, when he refused to be called the son of Pharaoh's daughter, but preserved it among the most cherished wishes of his heart, during his voluntary exile of forty years in the wilderness. "For all these things will I be inquired of by the house of Israel to do it for them." The disciples tarried at Jerusalem and continued with one accord in one place, in prayers and supplications, until the day of Pentecost was fully come.

The means which promote revivals, are not natural causes working uniformly, and invariably, producing the same results, but are week and wholly inefficient in themselves and dependent for their efficacy on the divine will. The gifts of the Holy Ghost are always "according to his own will." "God has chosen the weak things of the world to confound the things which are mighty." The gospel is the weakness of God, the excellency of the power is of him; hence the ministry is accountable for its fidelity, not for its success.

True revivals are attended with alarming apprehensions of sin and misery. "Felix trembled." The sermon of Peter sent a pang to the hearts of thousands. The inquiry, "men and brethren what shall we do?" expressed a strong emotion common and simultaneous among awakened sinners in that vast assembly. The jailor of Philippi, also, came trembling and astonished, and said, "sirs, what must I do to be saved." Though the outward expressions of inward emotions are modified by circumstances, and depend much upon the degree of knowledge, and upon the peculiar temperament of different individuals, yet, in all instances, the conviction of sin and misery is the same; every returning wanderer is led to smite his breast with the publican; to feel his want and to see that he must perish without a deliverer, and to return and to confess with tears, his unworthiness and poverty, with the prodigal; whatever attainments may have been made in piety and morality before, all, in any event, learn with Paul, to count all things but loss for the excellency of the knowledge of Christ Jesus our Lord, for whom they are ready to suffer the loss of all things, and they do count them dung, that they may win Christ and be found in him; not having their own righteousness, which is of the law, but that which is of the faith of the Son of God, the righteousness which is of God by faith.

The Mosaic ritual subserved its end and passed away.—Miracles were wrought, and confirmed the testimony which they were sent to establish, and ceased in the church; but there are other things inseparable from the uniform condition of our common humanity, and which are essential to the nature and perpetuity of the Gospel, and which must continue to the end of time: as for instance, man's ignorance of divine things, even when he has an intellectual acquaintance with them. Of the natural man, it must ever remain true, that he discerneth not the things of the Spirit of God, for they are foolishness unto him, neither can he know them, because they are spiritually discerned." Whenever the natural man, therefore, receives from the Holy Spirit, that illumination which discovers to him his sin and misery, and his need of a redeemer, this discovery must invariably be attended with emotion; he must become tremblingly alive to his guilt and danger, and the vast question which agitates him, must, in the very nature of things, take precedence of all others.— When we are threatened with the loss of property, or of kindred, or of liberty, whatever may be those calamities, merely temporal, which surround us, we can discover some alleviation, and gather courage from the hope of better days; but when the Holy Spirit convinces of sin, of righteousness, and of judgment, the evils which threaten us have neither measure nor mitigation; we fear and quake before a burning mountain, and the voice of unearthly words; we stand appalled and condemned in the presence of an offended God, and in view of the wrath to come. If we could pity ourselves as simply unfortunate, then we could remain strong amid unavoidable afflictions, and feel that we had merited a better fate; but when conscience turns accuser, and institutes a terrible scrutiny of the past, and brings up appalling visions of judgment and eternity, natural fortitude and resolution are of no avail. There is no waste, like that which wastes the supplies—no drain so exhausting, as that which exhausts the fountain—no blow, like that which smites the heart.— The spirit of a man can sustain his infirmity, but a wounded spirit, who can bear?

The miraculous changes, which a true revival of religion supposes, must be common to the church in all ages. They may extend to a few individuals, every month, for several years, as in the gathering of the churches of Corinth and Ephesus, or be a sudden and simultaneous influence upon thousands, in a moment, as in the great revival at Jerusalem; but all true revivals are the work of the Holy Ghost, who operates, in conjunction with the means of grace;" "whereby convincing, [either one, or thousands,] of their sin and misery, enlightening their minds in the knowledge of Christ, and renewing their wills, he doth persuade and enable them to embrace Jesus Christ, freely offered in the gospel."

Tradition affirms of Paul, that when he fulfilled his purpose of making a journey into Spain, he passed from Italy, on the old Roman road, across the Alps, which led him through Piedmont, where he paused and preached the gospel, and established a church. This secluded spot, remote from the corrupting influence of cities and false teachers, retained the primitive simplicity of the apostolic faith, unchanged, amid surrounding defection and apostacy. The churches which grew up here, were kept alive, from generation to generation, by influences graciously shed upon them from on high, until the seventh century, when they received accessions from other quarters. True Christians, throughout the Roman Empire, weary with remonstrating in vain against the corruptions of an apostate and a doomed church, and discouraged by opposition and persecution, retired, according to Moshiem, into an obscure place in the vallies of Piedmont. From the seventh to the twelfth centuries, we have repeated notices of them from their enemies; by them they are represented as maintaining a church state, separately from the church of Rome, and as existing and increasing, until they filled the beautiful and secluded vallies that lie embosmed amid the Alps and Pyrenees, with immense multitudes of believers in their unchanged and primitive creed. Though distinguished, from age to age, by the life and soundness of their Christianity, yet we know of no great movement among them, until near the close of the twelfth century. At that period, they were remarkably revived and spread themselves, and their peculiar opinions throughout the world. Intimately connected with the early progress of the primitive church, was the remarkable conversion of a young man, whose name was Saul, and whose education and position fitted him, preeminently, to be a chosen vessel, to be sent far from Jerusalem, among the Gentiles, to preach the unsearchable riches of Christ. A similar event was connected with the great work of grace, to which our attention is now turned. A rich merchant of Lyons, talented and educated, was present at a convivial meeting among his boon companions, when one of his friends, without any previous warning, suddenly expired, and went from the place of merriment to his last account.— The death of that man was a warning, never forgotten by the young tradesman—he became another man; he gave up his mercantile pursuits, distributed his property to the poor, and found peace in believing in that gospel which he discovered in his Latin testament. This he translated into French, and was soon surrounded by large congregations, and associated with other, and able ministers of Jesus, who, in conjunction with him, preached Christ with great earnestness and with great success. This merchant was Peter Waldo.— The Archbishop of Lyons, hearing of his doctrine and success, denounced him, and Pope Alexander the third, excommunicated him, devoting him and his followers to fire and sword. From Lyons he fled into Dauphiny, where he and his associates preached, and won great numbers to the faith. Driven from thence, he went into Picardy: a great revival attended his ministry, in that place; but assailed again by persecution, he fled into Germany, and finally settled in Bohemia. Through this beautiful country, his principles became speedily prevalent, and here, twenty years from the time of his conversion, he died in the triumphs of faith. During this period, the churches in the valleys were all in motion, partaking largely of divine influences, and their ministry penetrated into Spain, Italy, France, Germany, the Netherlands, Scotland, Ireland; in a word, into every nation of the Roman Empire, and spread their principles, and made converts every where. Reinerius Saccho declares in his report, as a Roman inquisitor, " that the sect was universally diffused, that there was no country in which they were not found in great numbers." Above a million were put to death, in France alone. The prisons were so crowded with them, other methods were devised and resorted to, to thin their ranks. The Inquisition was originated and established, to aid in their more speedy destruction; its infernal court followed them into every country, and wasted them under the forms of law. But even this process was too slow: crusaders, in vast armies, were employed by Pope Innocent the third, to exterminate them at once; these fell upon them in a war of indiscriminate cruelty and carnage: and the great revival was arrested in blood.

In the year 1503, a poor and comparatively friendless young man, the son of a miner, in the twentieth year of his age, and thirsting for knowledge, stood alone in the library of the University at Erfurth, and, while examining the title pages of books, he at length met with one entirely new to him. It was the Bible. This book he read with awakened interest; his frequent visits at the library were for the purpose of becoming acquainted with its contents. He is at length taken sick, and during his sickness, is filled with dreadful apprehensions of the wrath of God. He recovers and as he walks alone in the open field, he is overtaken by a storm—a thunderbolt plunges at his feet—he recoils from the smouldering chasm, falls upon his knees, and vows that if God will spare his life, he will devote it to his service. See him, then, according to the ideas of that day, fulfilling his vow in the habit of a monk, becoming a mendicant, and a recluse, and here, to use his own language, " I tormented myself to death, to procure for my troubled heart, and agitated conscience, peace in the presence of God," but in vain. The text, "the just shall live by faith," was deeply impressed upon his mind, and as he crossed the Alps, on his way to Rome, he fell sick, and, when at the point of death, the text again occurs to him, a great mental struggle ensues; he gains some faint knowledge of the great doctrine of justification—the battle-axe afterward in his hand against the walls of papal Rome—he recovers, and visits Italy, still intent on justification by the merit of good works. Here, while ascending Pilate's stair-case on his bended knees, a voice reaches his startled ear, the text occurs to him in a thunder peal, "the just shall live by faith." It was the voice of an effectual call; his will was renewed, his mind enlightened in the knowledge of the Redeemer, and he was enabled to embrace Jesus Christ, as he was freely offered in the gospel. Every monkish austerity had been essayed; he had fasted, prayed, and mortified his soul and body until, on one occasion, the light of his eye was quenched, and his worn and attenuated frame fell back lifeless on the floor of his cell, he was, with great difficulty recalled again to life, and hence he could say, if ever a monk went to heaven by his good works, I more; for where they fasted four weeks, I fasted seven, and excelled all in self-denial and in prayers, and in bodily mortifications. This man was Luther, an eminent preacher of total depravity; human impotence; effectual calling by the subjective and creative influence of the Holy Ghost; imputation, justification by faith in the righteousness of Christ; election and predestination. The light spread over all Europe, Switzerland, France, the Netherlands, Sweden, Denmark, Norway, England, Scotland, and Ireland, received the faith; whole nations threw off the Papal yoke, and vast multitudes continued to experience the power of that gospel which brought Luther to Christ. This is called the great reformation of the 16th century. Let us not, however, amid the controversies, and convulsions, and revolutions, of that age, lose sight of the great work of the Holy Ghost, whose gracious influences imparted, as we have seen, to Luther, were also imparted to thousands, and produced the same great results in them: they were in great numbers, convinced, as he was, of their "sin and misery, their minds were enlightened in the knowledge of Christ, their wills renewed, and they were persuaded and enabled to embrace Jesus Christ, as he was freely offered in the gospel." The reformation of the 16th century began and was spread by the Holy Ghost in the hearts of men; an irresistable spiritual influence descended in every country upon the people—men were everywhere pricked in the heart, awakened, convinced, and led to believe in the Lord Jesus Christ. The churches of the valleys hearing of the great revival, visited the reformers, and found, on a comparison of their respective views, that their opinions of church government, and of doctrinal and experimental religion, were the same; found that they were the same people, being perfectly joined together in the same mind, and in the same judgment. Calvin took his model of Presbyterianism from the Bohemians, which, two hundred years before, had been left them by Peter Waldo. Knox carried it into Scotland, and its General Assembly sent it into America. The churches of the valleys, are believed by Newton, Faber, Scott, and many others, and also by Old and New School Presbyterians generally, to be those witnesses in the wilderness who are referred to by St. John, in Revelations; and who are said by him, to have the word of God, and to bear the testimony of Jesus. The revival was according to this view of it, obviously divine—the great work of God. And in it, we may notice the following characteristics.

It was a revival of sound opinions—a return to the ancient faith. It was not a new discovery; a progress in the knowledge of God, such as had never been before enjoyed, but a return to the faith, once delivered to the saints.

It was in the next place a revival of their views in the way, not only of an intellectual conviction, but of an experimental acquaintance with the truth, so that the faith of the converts stood not in the wisdom of man, but in much assurance and in the Holy Ghost and in power. The advice of Luther to Spalatin, when he asked him what was the best method of studying the Scriptures, discovers to us the true secret of their confidence in the truth of their principles and why those principles became so generally prevalent and so mightily operative. "Hitherto worthy Spalatin, (said Luther) you have asked only things I was able to answer. But to guide you in the study of the Holy Scriptures is beyond my strength. However, if you insist on knowing my method, I will not conceal it from you."

"It is most plain we cannot attain to the understanding of Scripture either by study or by strength of intellect; therefore your first duty must be to begin with prayer. Entreat the Lord to deign to grant you, in his rich mercy, rightly to understand his word. There is no other interpreter of the word of God but the author of that word himself; even as He has said, 'They shall all be taught of God.' Hope nothing from your study, or the strength of your intellect; but simply put your trust in God, and in the guidance of his Spirit. Believe one who has made the trial of this method."

Men instructed and satisfied in their scruples, and enlightened in their knowledge, after this example, could not hold the truth in uncertainty, or in unrighteousness, but must have received it from the Spirit and under his purifying and subduing influences. A knowledge of the gospel, wherein the understanding and the heart, are fully pursuaded of its truth and sweetness, by the Holy Spirit, presupposes that the subjects of it, are already spiritual, that they have not only the form but the life and power of godliness. "Blessed art thou Simon Bar Jonah, for flesh and blood hath not revealed it unto thee but my father who is in heaven."

The means of grace in use were primitive. From the infinitely multipled new doctrines and new measures of Popery, all, turned back to the word of God, contained in the Scriptures of the Old and New Testaments, for their only and ever infallible rule of faith and practice ; and in this manner the Reformers became the propagators, not of a new religion, but of a faith once delivered to the saints, in its simplicity, purity and glory. No well informed New School man will pretend for a moment that the great revivals of the 13th and of the 16th centuries, were revivals of Pelagian opinions.— Luther and Melanchton, Zuingle and Calvin, yea the whole host of worthies from Peter Waldo to John Knox, condemned the errors of Pelagius, as included among the Papal abominations to be rejected and abhorred by every convert to the gospel. The confession of faith drawn up by the assembly of divines at Westminister, contains a beautiful epitome of their united testimony on the subject of doctrinal and experimental Christianity ; and hence we infer that a revival of Pelagianism is not a revival of true religion, but an apostacy from it.

The millenium, shall be a resurrection of the souls of those witnesses who were beheaded for the word of God and for the testimony of Jesus, in the same sense in which Elijah, arose from the dead, in the reproduction of his testimony and spirit, and power, in John the Baptist. As John was the facsimile of that ancient and venerable prophet in his austerity, preaching, zeal and faith, so the great reformations appearing at intervals, from the 13th to the 16th centuries, shall reappear, and the reformers long since dead, shall rise again, in the very countries moistened with the blood of their testimony, and renew their witness bearing in men who shall truthfully represent them, and successfully vindicated their honor and spread their opinions. The millenium, in other words, shall be a great revival of the doctrines, zeal, love, and piety of the martyrs and witnesses of Jesus. It shall differ in no respect, from the revivals of other days, but in one: they were partial and confined to small portions of the earth; this shall be universal—extend to all nations, and comprehend them all, in its blessed and transforming influences; all shall know the Lord from the least to the greatest. The religion of the millenium shall not be new in its doctrines, nor in its experimental nature and effects, but the same ancient faith received, experienced, and spread by the apostles, and reproduced and spread by a divine continuity and succession in doctrinal and vital godliness, and carried down to that blessed day, and then at once, or in a very brief period made universal.

True progress, I conclude therefore, will be backward to the old Christianity of the primitive churches, and to their identical faith, as set forth in the catechisms and primers and confessions of faith, of the martyrs and reformers and witnesses of Jesus in subsequent ages. The apostles, shall be enthroned in every true revival, in their despised and hated creed, and the rejected and murdered witnesses, shall be had in universal honor. The new divinity, being a most glaring and wide departure from the ancient faith, is undoubtedly an apostacy, not a progress—is a revival of false religion and not of the true, and it will never receive countenance, when Paul again rises from the dead, in the renewal of his testimony to the Romans, to the Galatians, to the Hebrews; when Waldo, and Wickliff, and Huss, and Luther, and Calvin, and Knox, when Latimer and Ridley and Rogers, when the whole army of the reformers rise again from the dead, and begin again effectually to spread those doctrines of grace, in the faithful propagation of which, they counted not their lives dear unto themselves. Finney, and Barnes, and Beman and Beecher, will surely make but a sorry appearance in the hands of these sons of Abraham. In them we shall see again exalted in power and in the Holy Ghost, and in much assurance, the great doctrines of election, of irresistable grace, of vicarious atonement, of original sin, and natural depravity, of justification, imputation and of human inability. In like manner as the Pharisees, received no countenance from Elijah when his principles, purity, and zeal, had a resurrection in John the Baptist, so shall the new divinity, receive no countenance when a revival of true religion shall appear again in the churches.

Many of these ancient worthies, have in Scotland, already broken the slumber of ages and the lids of their coffins ; have thrown aside their winding sheets, have renewed the vital current of their blood, and the vigor of their youthful days, and are again abroad to revive the testimony of the martyrs, and witnesses, of Jesus, and therefore mighty works do show forth themselves. Not only Erastian, but Pelagian error is fully condemned ; the gospel is preached in its primitive freedom and simplicity, the effect is truly cheering; the dead hear the voice of the Son of God and they that hear, live. It is indeed a revival of religion, in its truth, spirit, and power. The old Puritans of New England, also have broken the dreary silence of the church-yard ; they cannot rest in their graves. The liberalism and Pelagianism of their degenerate sons, make their bones ache in their coffins. Some have already made their appearance among the living, and the revival of their glorious gospel testimony is begun. The cry that their views are antiquated and that they are men far behind the age, is calculated to make them prominent and to arrest the attention of the church ; because the progress of the age is seen to be, not upward towards the mountain of the Lord's house, but downward from the blessed elevations of Mount Zion. And in our own beloved church, the revival has also commenced, the testimony of Jesus is extensively reproduced, the witnesses revive even in their recorded expositions of the faith, and their living voice is likewise extensively heard and honored. The new philosophy and new divinity have generally fallen into disrepute, and the inquiry now is for the old paths and the old way. No prospects of increasing numbers and wealth, will lead the Presbyterian Church to regret her solemn "act and testimony," and to take back again her disowned Synods, until she is previously convinced, that they have solemnly repudiated their errors and returned to the faith once delivered to the saints.

This revival is to a great extent, experimental, as well as doctrinal. I am acquainted with many in the ministry, who having been led partially astray by the new divinity, have again returned and have received the truth in greater assurance, than before their temporary wandering from the way, and I do certainly believe, that to as great an extent as in any church on earth, the ancient doctrine is received and preached, because its truth and beauty are seen and its sanctifying power is felt among us. If revivals of religion originate in connection with this blessed gospel, Old School Presbyterians, I confidently affirm, will be the last to question their genuineness.

But Mormonism has its revivals; *Christianism* has its revivals ; Popery has its revivals. False religion comes with all power, and signs, and lying wonders, and we are forced to discriminate: not to believe every spirit, but to try the spirits, whether they are of God. And if any man, as a professed teacher, come unto us, and bring not this doctrine, we are to inquire no farther; we are not to be influenced by the excellency of his character, or by the greatness of his parts; for Satan is talented, and transformed into an angel of light: no marvel, then, if his ministers are transformed, as the ministers of righteousness. If, therefore, any man come to us and bring not this doctrine, even the doctrine of our Lord Jesus Christ, we are not to receive him into our houses of worship, as a religious teacher, nor to bid him God-speed, as such, for he that biddeth him God-speed, by countenancing him, and furnishing him with credentials, is partaker of his evil deeds. We cannot believe that a revival of old heresies, a resurrection of Cerinthus, Arius, Pelagius and Socinus, in living representatives, in the churches, can be a revival of true religion. However much they may boast of their new discoveries, and superior sanctity, though they may compass sea and land to make proselytes, and surround themselves with new measures, and new converts, in great numbers, yet we have not so learned Christ, and are not to be deceived by specious appearances. When we see the Spirit undervalued and set aside, except in name, and the Son dishonored in his reconciliation, and depravity denied, and human ability, and men and measures exalted; the work of religious reformation, however wide-spread and imposing, is not of God, but is a fearful apostacy from a primitive christianity, and will end in popery, or infidelity, or in some other form of ultimate evil, to which it tends.

If it be urged, that during these seasons, there have been hitherto several genuine conversions to Christ, I reply, that it is because of the truth preached by faithful ministers, scattered among the false, and because of the soundness of the communicants, generally, in their prayers, experience, and conversation, during the progress of the excitement; and if these had been men of a different character, and had all taught and prayed in the true spirit of the new divinity, from the first commencement of the religious awakening, it would have been, from the beginning, worthless in its fruits. As soon, therefore, as a separation has been effected between the friends of the old, and new opinions, there has appeared also, an entire change in the character of the converts: the churches have became speedily filled with unrenewed men, who decry the gospel and its godly and conscientious defenders, and heap to themselves teachers, having itching ears.— The declension was never greater, in vital religion, than at the present moment, among all those who fully receive, and understandingly endorse the new divinity. It is the element of growing discord, and of inevitable decline and consumption. A true revival began here, eighteen years ago, but the new divinity revived with the old, and swept, like the mournful simoom, over the churches; before it—was the garden of Eden; behind it—life and verdure lie buried in the oblivion of a spiritual desert.

Neither in the apostolic ministry of the primitive church, nor among the witness-bearers in the wilderness, were there found, any, deemed good men and true, who affirmed that " Christ did not suffer the curse of the law, nor any part of it:" that imputed righteousness is a phrase which conveys no intelligible idea:" that "justice, in its common and appropriate sense, was not satisfied by the atonement;" that faith, irrespective of its relation to'" the righteousness of the Messiah," is reckoned for our righteousness: that original sin is false philosophy, and native depravity, an error of the schools: that man has ability to keep the law of God, without divine aid, can make himself a new heart, and does do it, whenever it is made: that subjective and almighty influences, in regeneration, break in upon the established laws of a moral government, and destroy its very nature, and that hence, regeneration is neither a miracle nor a mystery, but the simple persuasion of a man to correct his mistakes, and live a reformed life, and that, too, just in that degree in which these things lie within the compass of his natural, unassisted ability. No such doctrines were taught in the first century; but they were testified against, as destructive errors, by the Holy Apostles of the Lamb. No such doctrines were held by the witnesses of Jesus, in the wilderness; the three angels, who flew successively through the midst of heaven, having the everlasting gospel to preach to the slumbering nations, cried aloud against these ruinous delusions, until the shaft of persecution reached their hearts, and they folded their golden pinions, and sank down on Mt. Zion, with their eloquent voices choaked in blood. And whenever a revival of true religion again occurs, in any age, or country, they will again come to life, and rise, and fly, and bear again, unchanged, the same blessed and quickening evangelical testimony

The new divinity then, is another gospel, an apostacy from the faith, and the revivals connected with its progress, are revivals of a spurious christianity. However true it may be, that individuals do truly experience a saving change, during their temporary sway, yet the conversions were not wrought by the Holy Spirit, in view of the eroneous teachings, but in spite of their lethargic and soul destroying power. Did ever an apostle in language like the following, undervalue the work of the Spirit and say, "Not much less deluding, are the systems and tactics of those who fearing to invade the province of the Spirit, are careful to remind the sinner that he is utterly unable by his own unassisted powers, either to believe or to repent, to the saving of his soul. It might as truly be said that he cannot rise and walk by his own unassisted powers." (Duffield's work on Regeneration, p. 542.) Sentiments, such as these, they never uttered, nor did they countenance those that did, but with solemn awe and deep felt self abasement, they confessed, and denied not, that of themselves, they could do nothing, that to will was present with them, but that how to perform that which was good they found not, that when they were without strength in due time Christ died for the ungodly.— And as revivals of religion are produced in connection with the means of grace, by the supernatural power of the Holy Ghost, we may conclude justly, that those who make light of his indispensable agency, and maintain that men are fully able to repent and believe without it—decry those who revere his power and glory in the new creation, and that too, because they fear to take his glory from him, fear, "to invade the province of the Spirit"—that such men are far from resembling the apostles of the Lamb, and do as truly undervalue their views, as they undervalue ours.

Revivals of religion promoted by the utterance of such sentiments, in which men are told that, "if the sinner ever has a new heart, he must obey the command of the text, and go and make it himself." (Finney's sermons on important subjects, p. p. 18, 38.) That God "requires a service strictly according to our ability and to be measured by that, (that) he demands no more than our powers are fitted to produce, no more than we are able to render, (that) our obligations in all cases are limited by our ability," (Barnes' notes, 2 Cor. 8, 12.) Revivals of religion advanced by such instructions if they correspond in their character with the character of this new and strange gospel, will be revivals of natural religion merely, the work of man alone and not at all the work of the blessed and insulted Spirit. If faith is not the gift of God, not a principle implanted in the mind by the Holy Ghost by which we receive the righteousness of the Messiah, but an act of the mind, "If God promises, man believes, and this is the whole of it; (Barnes' notes) then the faith begotten in the revival, if it correspond with this view of its nature, is also the work of man; a merely natural, mental action. And this is equally true of repentance, and every other grace, if they are not the gracious productions of the Holy Ghost, but are the mere exercises of the natural heart, then the religion possessed by the new converts, is not spiritual, but natural, and it is as true of them as it ever was, that they are natural men still, and discern not the things of the spirit of God, and except they are born again, cannot see his kingdom. When men are told that they are not to *get* religion, not to experience it, not to *get* a new heart, but to love God with just such a heart as they now have, (i. e.) with the natural heart," that God requires a service strictly according to our ability and to be limited by that;" it is absurd under such a gospel to call the conversions, the work of the Spirit, the converts, spiritual and the revival, the work of the Holy Spirit, and for the plain reason, that its very promoters and the authorized expositors of its nature, convey a totally different idea, and maintain substantially, that it is the **work of man**, performed and limited by his natural ability.

When awakened sinners ask, what they shall do to be saved, and they are not told to seek for a new heart; for a supernatural change to be wrought in them by the Holy Ghost, and to connect them by faith with the justifying righteousness of Christ, but to resolve to serve God; and this resolution, or this governing purpose, is said to be a change of heart, and to be all that is required; sinners themselves are amazed at the breadth of the gate that leads to life, and the ease with which they can become christians. They had supposed before that the gate was strait, but this was in their simplicity, and under the old fashioned theology. They had been looking and praying for assistance from him, without whom, they had once been taught, "they could do nothing," but this they now have discovered was a great error, for they have now accomplished their regeneration with the utmost facility. They had hitherto looked beyond mere nature for help, and had depended on the Holy Ghost to enable them to repent and believe, but they have now learned that it might as truly be said, "that man could not arise and walk by his own unassisted powers," they could do, and had done, both the one and the other, in their own strength, they were really natural actions and easily put forth. Hence the revival is, in this aspect of it, not a revival of true religion, but a revival in men of an extraordinary self-complacency and self-reliance, and of contempt for the aid of the Holy Spirit. The inquiry room and the anxious seat, sufficiently harmless in themselves, and when employed for the sole purpose of convenient access to those who desire personal instruction and conversation, become, in these seasons, of spurious religious excitement, the principal places for effort against the doctrines of grace. Every objection raised by the awakened sinner, on the ground of his inability to change his own heart, is met by a denial of its truth; every objection raised on the ground of his dependence on the Holy Spirit, is met by a denial of such dependence, and he is required then, and there, to change his governing purpose, or to submit to God, which means in the mouths of these teachers the same thing, and when he consents to do it, the poor deluded creature is dedicated in a formal prayer, and in a most solemn manner to the Father, Son, and Spirit, as a child of God, and sent out in the capacity of a new convert, to convert others to the same delusion, to wonder at the great discoveries of modern times, at the width of the gate, and the breadth of the way, that leadeth unto life; and to be amazed at the stupidity of old-fashioned Presbyterians, and at his own former ignorance, in which he had erroneously supposed regeneration to be a supernatural change, and not a mere natural action, and performed with the utmost facility, and at a moment's warning by the creature himself.

Out of this view of the subject arises another, viz : that the ministry is responsible for its success, and that, if men had as much leisure all the year as they enjoy in the winter season revivals might be perpetuated throughout the year, and in any event, they can be produced at pleasure by the church; and with these low views of revivals the opinion is, doubtless, correct. It needs, but to commence a protracted meeting for the purpose, and then systematically to assail the old theology, respecting human inability and depravity, and to convince the hearers that a resolution to serve God is regeneration, and that each one can change his heart as easily as he can rise and walk, and if the community have not been too frequently assailed and deceived in this way, the usual phenomena will follow, and protestants will abound in all the outward semblances of religion, and work as earnestly to enter heaven in the use of the new measures, and by their own righteousness, as the Romanists. But great revivals of religion in which the work of the Son and Spirit are set aside excepting in name, and men and measures are exalted and made to occupy their places—are not the blessed, and powerful, and purifying workings of the Holy Spirit; and in the midst of them it behoves us to attend to the Apostolic admonition' " Beloved, believe not every spirit, but try the spirits whether they be of God, for many false prophets are going out into the world."

It will be seen, then, that our objections are not against the New School, because they hold meetings which last several days. The meeting of Hezekiah was protracted. Protracted meetings are very common among Old School Presbyterians, at their sacramental services, and have frequently been attended with revivals of a marked and desirable character—Revivals, in which the doctrines of total depravity, human inability, imputation, atonement, election, and, in fine, in which all the leading doctrines of the gospel were fully and ably exhibited and defended. It is not the continuance of a meeting through several successive days, against which we object, but it is the denial of the gospel, and the spread of error, and the ruin of souls by this means, which awakens our regret, and calls forth our solemn remonstrance against those whose deceived heart hath turned them aside.

Old Schoolism, and a Laodecean indifference to all religion, have come in many quarters to signify substantially the same thing. It is not, however, the zeal of those who compass sea and land, to make proselytes, but the errors which they so industriously spread, against which we testify. It is good always to be zealously affected in a good thing, but great talent, zeal and effort expended in subverting whole churches, and in the dissemination of fatal error, is a melancholy spectacle to look upon, and he that loves the master and the souls of men will not be able to hold his peace, even though he may be sure, for years, to be extensively misunderstood by his friends, and bitterly denounced by his enemies.

We, then, are not opposed to zeal in the cause of Christ. The love of Christ constraineth us: a friend may bear with a friend's infirmities, and die in his defence, but Christ bears with his imbittered foes; bears with their vile reproach, encounters their scorn and rage, and sinks with a broken heart, and in bloody agony to the grave, to deliver them from death and hell; and can we, whose sins were laid upon him, be indifferent to a love like this? Even the hardened Saul was overcome by the kindness of David; and can we remain indifferent to a love which infinitely surpasses the love of David? Can we turn, in cold neglect, from the garden and the cross, from scenes which affected the material universe, and made the stones to cry out; and act in accordance with those laws of spiritual life which are implanted by the Holy Spirit deep in the christian nature? Nay—the emotions of love and gratitude are spontaneous and irrepressible; they swim in the moistened eye, and throb in the strong sympathies of the renovated heart. Who among us, therefore, believing, as we do, respecting the love of Christ, can enter the desk, and exchange the inspiration of the christian, for the coolness of a philosopher, and deliberately show how little Christ has done for us, when we believe that he meets every want, relieves every difficulty, bears every burden, and comprehends, in his finished work, our eternal redemption. Others may do this—may speak disparagingly of him—may represent that, he *"merely"* did this, and *"barely"* did that—may move on without emotion, in every discourse respecting Jesus, be as dull as lead and as cold and cheerless, to listening disciples, as the moonlit shadows of the cemetery that steal into the vaults and sleep upon the pale faces of the dead; but can we, who make Christ all, and in all, pursue a course so inconsistent with our views of his wonderful and affecting relations to us, and of our infinite debt of gratitude to him? Others may deny that he bore the curse of the law; that he wrought for us a justifying righteousness; may deny original sin and natural depravity; discourse of human ability and measure obligation by it; represent a change of heart, to be a change of purpose; christianity to be purely intellectual, a stranger and an enemy to the emotions; and may depend upon exciting tales, and measures, and human appliances, and the fears of hell, to ensure success, and to surround themselves with followers; but God forbid that we should glory, save in the cross of our Lord Jesus Christ. Those who depend upon human ability, and the horrors of hell, without the cross, may make converts, but will they be instrumental in making men christians? Ham, was not restrained from making a mock at sin by a wrath that swept fifteen cubits above the loftiest mountains. The shower of fire, enraged with brimstone, did not make the daughters of Lot chaste. Idolators, were not restrained from their infernal orgies, and sacrifices, and revellings; even when Sinai was all on fire, and the everlasting mountains were scattered, and the perpetual hills did bow. The tents of Cushan were in affliction; the curtains of the land of Midian did tremble; the lips of even the hardened Pharoah quivered at the voice of God, and rottenness entered into the bones of the brave around him, amid those appalling visitations which filled a kingdom with alarm and despair, yet still omnipotence is pursued by these very men and defied, in the very heart of that sea, which had uttered its voice at the awful *presence*, and lifted up its hands on high. The bolt of heaven may plunge upon the face of the rock, on the mountain's brow, and send its smouldering fragments to the vale below, but though broken, it will remain adamant still : terror may break the courage, but it cannot melt the heart. Popery can open the crater of her purgatory and bring back the death wail of the departed to the ears of the living, and drain the coffers of princes, and the purses of the peasantry, among otherwise enlightened nations; but it cannot close the door of the brothel, nor purify and elevate a kingdom which is full of darkness. Men will go from their gloomiest reveries of hell to sport with their own deceivings, to kiss the mouth of the pit, and to wanton with fire and death: nothing will avail except Christ be created in them the hope of glory. They may be trained to part with wealth, to sleep in sackcloth; to ascend Pilate's staircase on their knees; to go on pilgrimages; to take the vows of celibacy, and of poverty; to take the anxious seat; to kneel in the mire; and to compass sea and land to make one proselyte; but a religion without the cross, whether Papal or Protestant, is a body without a soul. We, therefore, preach Christ "crucified; to the Jews, a stumbling block; and to the Greeks, foolishness; but to every one that believeth the power of God, and the wisdom of God. The gospel is indispensable; without it the law can be of no avail. It is not our complaint, therefore, that the New School have too much zeal in preaching Christ; on the contrary, we are often oppressed with the painful apprehension that they do not preach him at all. If they preached Christ everywhere, spake with the tongues of men, and of angels, and moved the stones to cry out from the walls of their churches, and the beam from the timber to answer it, and to shame the moral insensibility of their hearers, and if thousands were pricked in the heart, and cried, men and brethren, what must we do to be saved, and repented and believed the gospel, let our right hand forget its cunning, and our tongue cleave to the roof of our mouth, if we would gainsay them.

Nor do we believe that ministers can watch with too great diligence, and with too tender a solicitude for the souls of their hearers, as those that must give account. When we have respect to the worth of the soul, and see unrenewed multitudes, just at the parting point between two eternities; some constantly ascending to the ravishing delights of Eden, and others constantly descending, "to groan, where their groanings end not, to sigh, where their sighs do always sigh, and to weep where their tears do always fall and always weep; but not in mercy's sight," we may well have "great heaviness and continual sorrow in our hearts," and "warn every man, night and day, with tears." If accused of fanaticism, or madness, it would be a sufficient vindication to say, "if we are beside ourselves at the danger encountered by those who sport on the crumbling verge of the bottomless pit;" it is for your sakes, because we know you cannot abide the wrath you provoke; because we would win you back from gaining such infinite harm and loss. Other losses may be repaired—this never. The winding-sheet of a ruined soul is made from the iron folds of a miserable eternity. The grave of a lost spirit is a yawning hell; its companion, despair; its worm, dieth not; its fire is never quenched. Xerxes beheld his army in living masses, crowding the plains around him, and stretching far as his eye could reach, and wept when he thought how soon that mighty host would become powerless, and their formidable ranks be broken and buried in the oblivion of the grave. And a greater than he beheld the city, beautiful for situation, and teeming with life and thought how soon it would be wasted without inhabitant, and its guilty children buried underneath its subverted walls, and descending towers, and wept, and said, "oh, that thou hadst known, even thou, in this thy day, the things that belong to thy peace, but now they are forever hid from thine eyes;" and may we not have tears to shed, and consistently join in the lamentation over the millions who are ready to perish?

It is not, then, because men weep over the ruins of the fall, and abound in warning their hearers of approaching wrath, and in expostulations, and appeals, and efforts to turn them from their destrctive ways; this is a course justfiable when properly regulated, and highly commendable in every minister of Christ; "Knowing, therefore, the terrors of the Lord, we also persuade men:" but when, in their zeal to save, they destroy, grieve and dishonor the Spirit, in his work, set aside the institution of justice, and the principal glory of the cross in honoring it, their very successes give us pain, and we cannot but regard their instructions, and their highly popular works on regeneration and atonement, and their notes on the Bible, as a sad aggregate of evil influences, destined to operate widely and permanently, in strengthening and perpetuating the very woes, which their misguided authors intended to prevent and remove. The course of error is ever progressive; its successive converts ultimately turn its early twilight into intense darkness. The generations that rise, and become educated in the opinions of Duffield, Beman, Barnes, and Finney, will not tarry long in the sight of their more sober masters, but will find their way to a distance from the gospel, far more dreary and hopeless than they. The evil is already at work, and will mark out for itself its own highway of ruin. Those who have given it its origin and tendency, cannot control or direct its progress: error is the loosened avalanche; it *will* reach the vale below, and those who put it in motion, however much they may subsequently regret the course they have taken, cannot arrest it, midway, till the endangered and trembling villager can make his escape,—its plunge is downward, accelerated and remorseless,—its resting-place is in blood.

It is not, then, matter of regret with us, to see the votaries of ambition, and wealth, and fashion, and pleasure, pause, and turn pale, and become filled with remorse for the past, and fears for the future, and quit their pursuits, for days together, to attend to the interests of their souls. A king did this, and his courtiers and his subjects followed his example, in a solemn fast of three days, because God had said, "in forty days, and Ninevah shall be destroyed;" and we should rejoice to see cities and nations again follow that example, and men forget to labor, and forget to eat their bread; and ships ride at anchor, unmaned, and shops close along the streets of crowded cities, and the plough and the spade lie still, and the hum of business, and the song of the reaper, over whole countries, become hushed in a Sabbath stillness, and nations be born in a day. It is not in the fact, that men attempt to flee from the wrath to come, but in the fact that their souls are in peril, when they do flee, in consequence of the instructions which depreciate the only remedy, and throw them back upon their own resources for salvation; it is not because they are pointed to the bleeding cross, as prisoners of hope, but because they are turned away from it: it is not because they are assured, that they must be born again, but because they are assured that they do not need a change of nature, but only a change of purpose. It is, in a word, because upon all the vital questions of Christianity, the truth is mixed with fatal error, that we cannot experience those emotions of unmingled joy, which we should have felt, were men to abandon their philosophy, and to preach the gospel. This would awaken confidence in their labor, and joy unspeakable over their success.

We object then, to the revivals under the preaching of the new divinity, not because they are revivals of true religion, for in these we sincerely rejoice, but because they have so many marks of spuriousness—so many evidences that they are the mere result of exciting measures and anecdotes—the work of man, and not the work of God. The reasons for this judgment have been already given, I will now close with a summary statement of them.

1. They are a revival of old heresies, against which the spirit testified in the apostolic ministry, and in the martyrs, and reformers, who had the word of God, and the testimony of Jesus. They revive the heresy that "Christ did not suffer the curse of the law, nor any part of it, and that he has not obeyed the law vicariously." This is an old Jewish heresy, revived afterward by Arius, in the north, and by Mahomet in the south, and by Socinius, in the sixteenth century.

2. They deny original sin, and native depravity, and maintain the ability of man to keep the law of God in his own strength and without the aid of the spirit, and thus revive the old heresy of the Pharisees, and of Pelagius and of the

Papists, on these points. The scroll on which these errors are written, never had the image and superscription of the Son; it is destined to the flames; the Lord shall consume it with the breath of his mouth, and destroy it with the brigtness of his coming. The revival of these heresies is not of God, but a sad apostacy; and however they may be for a time sustained, by all power, and signs, and imposing appearances, they will in the end, increase unto more ungodliness.

3 They are not the result of divine influences; because God does not renew and sanctify by means of error, but with the truth as it is in Jesus; and because the authors of them, in several ways, indirectly at least, teach us, that they are, or may be, the work of man, as for instance :—

First. In teaching that a supernatural agency is not necessary to produce them. "God," says Mr. Barnes, "requires a service strictly according to our ability, and to be measured by that." Duffield teaches that the sinner no more requires the Holy Spirit to enable him to beleive and repent, than he requires his agency to enable him to arise and walk. Mr. Finney says that "if the sinner wants a new heart, he must go and make it himself." A revival of religion originated and conducted on these principles, is human, because it brings man to himself,—to his own resources for redemption, and not exclusively to God in whom alone is his help.

Second. In maintaining that regeneration is neither "a mystery, nor a miracle," but that it is effected by moral suasion, in which God does nothing for man, that he cannot and is not finally persuaded to do for himself; the change is easily and readily wrought, it is effected by the sinner in view of motives, and without any more, or other assistance than is given him in the performance of any natural action. There are no new principles imparted by the Spirit other than there is to a drunkard when he is made into a sober man; *he* is a new creature; the change is sufficiently great to justify this language, and so it is in this new kind of regeneration.

A new divinity revival is therefore wholly the work of man, or it is as much so, and in the same sense as plowing, sowing, reaping, and joining temperance societies, is the work of man. Men are induced to do these things in their natural strength and in view of motives, and in the same manner they are induced to regenerate themselves.

Third. In teaching that faith, and repentance are not the gift of God. That no new heart is communicated, no life imparted to the sinner, the principle of which he did not have before, and could not originate of himself, and at any time without the aid of the Holy Spirit, for this according to them would be to hold that man was physically depraved, physically unable to obey God and therefore under no obligation to do it " and none but a tyrant" could demand it of him. A revival in which these errors revive, and that fashions itself according to these instructions cannot be the work of the Spirit, but is a revival of old heresies, the result of natural ability for which we can feel no veneration, in which we can repose no confidence, and which carries on all its features the signs of its antichristian origin, of its earthly, sensual, and ruinous tendencies. Beloved, believe not every Spirit, but try the spirits whether they be of God.

CHAPTER VIII.

DOCTRINAL DIFFERENCES CONTINUED.

Tendencies of the new divinity—The new divinity rests upon one or at most two assumptions, both of which are false—Tends to infidelity.

Great apostacies are not the growth of a day ; they do not reach their maturity at once, but like the leprosy commencing at the extremities, and farthest from the seat of life, they spread gradually until they extend through the whole system. About two hundred years before the beginning of the Christian era, the belief became prevalent that Moses delivered two codes of laws, from Mount Sinai to the Hebrews. One in writing, and the other orally. And when our Lord appeared on the earth, the oral had come to be regarded as of higher authority than the written law. The insignificant tradition had in two centuries obtained a giant growth, and had "made void the law of God." Math. xv. 6.

The celibacy of the clergy was introduced gradually, and from the smallest beginnings. It was at first voluntary ; then it came to be admired as the highest evidence of personal purity ; the brightest ornament of Christian character. Afterward it passed into a law and the ministry were "forbidden to marry."

The merit of good works, that vast mint of Rome, in which she coins all her gold, and by which she opens a drain upon the wealth of nations, is a dogma which arose from her doctrines of ability, and uncommanded duties. Her saints did all, and even more, than was required in the word of God, and then followed penances, pilgrimages, purgatory, absolutions, and indulgences, until a rapacious priest-hood kept guard, in the imaginations of the people, at the gates of Pandemonium, and shut up, or liberated at their pleasure the souls of the departed.

I need not however, multiply instances, to show that the decline of churches is gradual, and their apostacy insidious and unexpected. It is like the breach of waters, drop by drop it oozes out, and frets and wears and widens its channel, until its rush is like the sea.

We have met with a treatise on the nature of virtue, in which the venerable author attempts indepenently of divine revelation, to build up a theory on this subject, which by its correspondence with the word of God, would discover to us the reasonableness of the divine law. In this theory, he teaches, that disinterested benevolence is the sum of all virtue, and selfishness, the sum of all sin, and here he left it, and died without discovering that it was a theory at variance with every other part of his own most excellent system of theology.

Dr. Hopkins, and Dr. Emmons, took up this error, assuming it to be a primary and incontrovertable truth, and followed it out in some of its affinities, and instead of teaching according to the blessed gospel, that "God was in Christ, reconciling the world unto himself, not imputing their trespasses unto them," (2 Cor. v. 19.) taught that God required disinterested benevolence, or such a love to God as would lead us to be willing for his glory to be his enemy forever, and such a love for our neighbor, as would lead us to be willing to take his place in hell. Along these extreme lines of separation, from the simplicity of truth, many have in consequence frequently wasted a worse than barren ministry, and have taught themselves and their hearers, that these hideous metaphysical creations, were of the very essence of true religion, whereas scarcely any thing could have been conceived, which could have been more directly opposite to its glorious nature. The Apostles taught, that men should believe in a God, reconciled in Christ; but they taught that men must submit to an absolute God. The former taught, that men must be willing to be saved through a Redeemer, but the latter, that they must be willing to be damned in order to salvation.

Dr. Edwards, the younger, took up the same original error, on the nature of virtue; and dividing justice into three parts, distributive, commutative, and public, made the atonement of Christ to meet the claims of the latter only, and to be a mere matter of governmental utility and safety, or a grand manifestation of disinterested benevolence.

Dr. Taylor and Mr. Finney, starting also at the same point of departure, and following out the same error, into the new affinities of which its prolific nature is capable, are beginning to wander on the frigid confines of Socinianism, and have already entered into some of the worst forms of that apostacy.

After this manner, an error apparently harmless at the first, and scarcely one hundred years old, and originating with a sound divine, and one of the greatest and best of men, has been gradually, and in various directions, evolving different and cardinal errors, which have ultimately mingled and spread into vast systems, and which now float, with their dark, pestilential vapors, upon Mount Zion, distributing every where the elements of decline and death.

Take, for example, the New School errors on atonement, and turn back upon their source, and we find them all flowing from a single fountain. They all have a metaphysical, not a biblical origin; they grow from philosphy, falsely so called, and not from the inspirations of the Holy Ghost. "There is a third sense in which the term justice, is frequently used, and the consideration of which, will lead us directly to the nature of that satisfaction which Jesus Christ has made for sinners. We mean, what is commonly denominated general, or public justice. In order to distinguish it, both from pecuniary and legal justice, it has been called moral justice. In this acceptation, it has no direct reference to law, but embraces those principles of virtue or benevolence, by which we are bound to govern our conduct, and by which God himself governs the universe." "In introducing this system of mercy, which involved a suspension of the penal curse, God has required a satisfaction to the principles of public or general justice." (See Beman on atonement, pp. 132—133.)

The atonement, according to Dr. Beman, therefore, satisfies, not the law of God, but the principle of benevolence, and this principle, he affirms, has no direct reference to law. On this point, the whole system of the new divinity hinges and swings. Through this gateway, it pours its legions on the church of God. The system has found, in the doctrine of disinterested benevolence, a first principle, an eternal and an immutable truth, and it boasts and swaggers, and hardens itself against the testimony of Jesus. Its visitations are dreaful; the out pourings of ever accumulating evils. It loses all veneration, and as it is endorsed by a great name, and claims to be a first principle; it assumes that it cannot be wrong, and it assails, without any misgivings, whatsoever may fall in its way. Violated law, and injured justice, according to it, and in direct contradiction to the views of President Edwards, its original author, are never satisfied. Over the dishonored precepts of the one, and the broken sceptre of the other, the truly guilty are permitted to pass with impunity, and to profane with their unhallowed presence, the diamond pavement that glitters around the throne of God. The garden, the cross, the resurrection morn, are turned by it, into the enduring memorials of a successful conspiracy, in which justice was evaded, and the penalty of her holy law suspended forever: in which righteousness and peace parted, to meet no more—truth and mercy, to embrace no more. They were separated at the fall by the sin of man—at the cross by a conspiracy, and in glory, by a dispensation. "The law can have no penal demand, except against the offender; with a substitute it has no concern, though a thousand substitues should die, the law, in itself considered, and left to its own natural operation, would have the same demand on the transgressor, which it always had. This claim can never be invalidated this penal demand can never be extinguished;" (Beman on Atonement, p. 99.) To the heavenly blessedness, Paul has no title, and no right; justice has claims still upon him, and forever fixes on him her consuming gaze, and forever demands his blood. Truth is also offended at his guilty presence, and utters against him her dreadful maledictions, and forever demands his exclusion from that holy place; and there is war, in heaven, not between obedient and disobedient angels, but in the very bosom of infinite purity itself. Paul is saved, but the attributes of God are set at perpetual variance with each other. "Behold how great a matter a little fire kindleth."

If the "love of being in general;" or benevolence is the sum of all virtue, and selfishness the sum of all sin; then no moral distinctions can exist back of intelligent mental preferences, and neither holiness, or sin, can belong to the nature of a moral being, but must always belong to his acts. And then nature loses nothing by ordinary generation, gains nothing by regeneration. Sin, therefore, is disobedience in all instances, and can in no case be a mere "want of conformity to law;" and regeneration is obedience, and not the implantation of a new principle in the soul; and faith and repentance and love do not proceed from any such new principle created by the Holy Spirit, but they are acts performed by ourselves in view of motives. Love to God, also, flows not from a new heart, but from the natural heart; the same heart, in all respects, with which we loved sin. The direction and the object of the love are changed, but not the heart; and faith is an act of man, not "the gift of God," not a principle implanted in the soul by which we are brought into a living union with Jesus Christ, but the same exercise in every respect, with which we believe any proposition, differing, specifically in nothing, but in the things believed.

And this, according to the theory which we oppose, is made to be true of all the graces of the spirit; they are purely natural actions; the simple unchanged outgoings of those natural qualities with which we are born and enter the world. Regeneration is, hence, neither a mystery, nor a miracle, but purely an exercise of the natural heart, performed in the ordinary manner, and with the carnal mind; and the natural man discerns the things of the Spirit of God, and the carnal mind loves God, and that which is born of flesh is faultless in itself, and can please God. Infants, also, can have no moral character, because they have not yet put forth those intelligent preferences on which the moral character depends, and hence they cannot be as yet the subjects of the moral government of God. They cannot be renewed by the Holy Ghost, for they have no sinful nature to be renewed, not washed in the blood of Christ, for they have no sin to wash away; they are mere animals, die by the same law, and perish in the same oblivion. God is the God of Abraham's seed in their infant state, in the same sense in which he is the God of the offspring of the beast that perish; for infants are not moral agents, and there is nothing in the ordinance of baptism, or in the promises to believing parents, which can possibly raise them in the scale of being to that high dignity, before they shall have put forth an intelligent moral preference: a moral being cannot be created even by omnipotence, he must create himself.

Accordingly, the church has, in all past ages, been involved in a great error on this subject, and has attributed to the Holy Spirit far greater part in the matter of our redemption than he ever performed, and a power and glory which were not his due. Indeed, the reasons for his special dispensation are not very obvious, since all which he ever accomplished, could have been effected without his agency altogether, or at least he merely persuades men to do what they could have easily done before, and which things they at length actually do accomplish themselves, and that, without previously receiving from him any new principle of spiritual life. And when this point is gained, is the next step in the departure from the truth either singular or difficult? To deny his person altogether? For if we can take away from him all his appropriately official work, and cover his glorious ministration with dishonor, will it be at all astonishing if, finally, we do not so much as know "whether there be any Holy Ghost?"

But the error denies the holiness of God's nature also, and degrades him from the glory of his eternal thrown to the condition of a mere subject. The law by which his conduct is regulated, and his character determined, is that of benevolence. This law, as it is reported, graduates its requirments by the abilities of moral beings. While it requires no *more* than they can render, it still requires *all* that they can render, and of God it requires infinite benevolence, because he is infinite; he never can exceed its claims, neither in himself, nor in the person of his Son, for "Jesus Christ was bound to obey the law for himself, and could no more perform works of supererogation, or obey on our account, than any body else." (See Lectures to Professing Christians, pp. 215, 216.) Imputed righteousness would, therefore, be an impossibility, because that which Jesus Christ owed for his own justification, as a natural subject, could justify no one but himself.

Thus, by the issues of a metaphysical subtlety, is the church deprived of the Spirit's inward and purifying graces and of a Saviour's outward and justifying righteousness. In following it, the only infallible guide has been abandoned, the only spot on earth, in which the new creation reposes in living verdure ; and as we advance, the rose of Sharon and

and the lily of the valley lift up their beautious heads no more beneath the sunny skies of a perpetual spring. The regions which we approach, grow dreary and more dreary still, until spiritual life itself becomes extinct and a perpetual winter asserts its gloomy reign.

The doctrine of man's ability to keep the law of God perfectly in this life, appears also to hold an affiliated relation to the original error on the nature of virtue, for it allows no character to a moral nature, but only to an intelligent moral preference ; nature, therefore, must be mere capacity : and obligation, must be measured by its *strength*, and *character* determined by its actings: and as the law requires perfect obedience, the ability must necessarily exist to obey it; in the language of Mr. Barnes, "our obligations in all cases are limited by our ability." (Notes 2 Cor. viii. 12.) The ability must be plenary, or else it is not an ability ; if there is the least defect in it, if every element which appropriately enters into the idea of ability, does not exist in fallen man, then it cannot be said of him, that he is able to keep the law of God, for the ability to keep the law, to be any thing at all, must be altogether, and in every respect, adequate to that end. "None but a tyrant demands more than can be rendered, and to demand more, is the appropriate description of a tyrant." (Notes of Mr. Barnes, 2 Cor. viii. 12.)

Accordingly what can be more legitimate than the conclusion at which Mr. Finney has at length arrived. That men really do that which they are perfectly able to do : at least some of them keep the law of God perfectly in this life. Would it not be a most singular and most unaccountable result, that among the millions of our race not one had yet been found who had done what each individual among men could as easily have done without supernatural aid as he could have used his power to "arise and walk?" Granting the premises, assumed in the New School divinity to be correct, then Mr. Finney's conclusion is also correct, and he is far more consistent, than those who start with him in his premises and then refuse to follow him in his just and irresistable conclusions. The starting point of Mr. Finney, and his New School antagonists, is the same. The self same dark stream which bears his barque, bears theirs to the same stygian pool; and though they may pause in terror and tie up their boat, and cry out against him for his temerity, in keeping on his way, yet whenever they break from their own moorings, they must inevitably follow in his wake. While they maintain that man in his natural state, and without supernatural aid can at any moment, keep the law of God perfectly, Mr. Finney, should not be decried by them and excluded from their pulpits, for maintaining the very logical conclusion, that some men at least, do keep the law of God perfectly, inasmuch as they have confessedly the additional aid afforded them by the infinite motives of the gospel. Moreover, if obligation and ability, limit and govern each other, if the law does not require of man, in his fallen state, all that it did require of him, in his state of primeval innocence and purity, but is modified in its claims, and adapts itself to the weakness of his present condition, if the command, "Thou shalt love the Lord thy God with all thy heart, and with all thy soul, and with all thy mind, and with all thy strength,"—(Mat. xii. 30,) signifies merely that you shall love God with your heart as it now is, and does not have respect both to the purity of the principle from which the love is required to flow and to the act itself—if in a word, the claims of the law are to be regulated by the existing and ever fluctuating ability of sinners, then the following positions can be maintained:

Saul of Tarsus, who thought verily that he ought to do many things contrary to the name of Jesus of Nazareth," (Acts xxvi. 9,) was not sinful for being in that state and for acting accordingly, but for those sinful and voluntary acts which brought him into it. And his subsequent sorrow and deep repentance, and many tears, on account of his persecutions of the church, were rather the evidences of a weak conscience, than of a truly gracious state.

The same is true, also, of the inebriate; the several acts which bring him into a state of beastly insensibility, are sinful, but the state itself is not; for in it he has lost the ability to be holy, and when ability is lost, the obligation is destroyed. It cannot, therefore, be affirmed that drunkenness is itself sinful, on this theory, any more than extension and impenetrability can be said to be the sins of a board. It surely will not be maintained that the drunken man can now, on the instant, throw off his lethergy, and put forth "the governing purpose" of sobriety—and of consequence he has for the time being, succeeded perfectly in destroying the claims of the divine law. This state he can perpetuate at his pleasure, and can cease, for years, to be a subject of the moral government of God; for "our obligations, in all cases, are limited by our ability; this is obviously the rule of equity." "None but a tyrant ever demands more than can be rendered, and to demand more, is the appropriate description of a tyrant." (B. Notes, 2 Cor. viii.)

The same is true, with regard to fallen angels and lost spirits in the prison of woe; in that dark abode, love is excluded by perfected enmity, and hope, by perfected dispair; there the inability to love God, is entire and unending, and capable of being overcome by omnipotence alone. And if the law, measures its claims by the ability of its subjects, it certainly can have no claims upon the damned, and they likewise, are absolutely and forever, released from the moral government of God. All the millions belonging to the period of infancy, must be included in the same catagory, with all those who have by their subsequent voluntary acts, placed themselves in a condition of real inability to keep the law by either the temporary want or the final loss of all ability to obey it.

In this manner does this single error make void the law of God, not only by admitting sinners to the glory of heaven, without meeting and magnifying its righteous claims through the vicarious obedience of Christ, but also by measuring those claims by a rule, as false in its nature, as it is demoralizing in its tendencies ; a rule which makes obligation to decrease with the increase of actual wickedness, among all the guilty beings that people the universe.

The doctrine of ability, as held by the New School, cannot be maintained, even by the very analogies to which they so confidently resort, in its illustration and defence ; for what has the inability of a man to lift a mountain, to do with his inability to love God? The former was never a moral obligation, and never could be one; the latter is a moral obligation, and its strength can never be impaired. The inability in the two cases resemble each other only in their degrees, but they differ wholly from each other, because they differ in their natures. The one belongs to physics, the other to ethics; the one is an inability of bones and sinews, the other of a moral nature. But take an instance more strictly analogous, to wit: the inability of a debtor to pay his debts, and does this inability, though equal in degree with his inability to lift a mountain, cancel his obligations? no, certainly not, for it differs from the former in kind; man was never under moral obligation to lift a mountain, but he was always under obligation to fulfill his covenant engagements ; the latter obligation is moral, and perpetuates itself by a necessary law ; it can never be impaired by any loss of ability, whatever, and hence the whole system is seen to be essentially false, and cannot plead a single appropriate analogy in its defence.

The reiterated assertions of Mr. Barnes and others, that an inability is physical, whenever it is *real*, is calculated to deceive those who cannot comprehend their meaning, but no others. The inability of fallen angels and of fallen man, to love God, in their own unaided strength, is as real, and as great in degree, as their inability to create a world ; but these two kinds of inability differ totally and infinitely from each other. The reality of the inability to love God, does not make it physical, any more truly, than it makes it chemical, or agricultural; the inability of God to lie, is real and substantial; in other words, it is absolute and infinite; but is not therefore physical, and as destitute of moral character, as the inability of the sun to shed darkness on the earth. The inability, in both instances, is equally a reality; but they differ infinitely from each other, because the former is the inability of a moral being to do evil, and the latter, the inability of matter to violate the laws which are impressed upon it.— Our inability to create a world, belongs to our physical constitution ; our inability to love God, to our moral constitution. The former has no moral character, whatever, the latter is wholly sinful. The absoluteness of the inability to create a world, renders criminality impossible ; the absoluteness of the inability to love God, renders criminality infinite. In the former instance, the inability is an excuse ; in the latter, a crime.

God is one, and his law is one, presenting forever the same unvarying aspect, and putting forth forever the same high and holy claims ; no weakness of depraved nature, can possibly weaken its original integrity. The trembling "debtor, to do the whole law," (Gal. v. 3,) the mere wreck of what his nature once was, hears the same voice from the burning throne, which rings in the ear of a seraph, "pay me that thou owest;" and the same finger which traced its precepts, amid fire and darkness, on the enduring rock, writes out the doom of inability on the gates of hell, "verily I say unto thee, thou shalt by no means come out thence, till thou hast paid the uttermost farthing," (Math. v. 20.) Inability can, among no intelligences, no where, in no worlds, deliver from its stern dominion, or break the arm of its power, and hence we can say with peculiar emphasis and truth, "man's inabili-

TENDENCIES OF ERROR. 197

is God's opportunity;" for if there had been a law given, which could have given life, verily, righteousness should have been by the law, (Gal. iii. 21.)

Again, it is maintained, as another result, that if ability to obey is essential to obligation, and intelligent preferences essential to character, then the moral government of God is exclusively a government of motives, and omnipotence cannot prevent sin. "Free moral agents can do wrong under all possible preventing motives," (See Christian Spectator, Sept. 1830, p. 503.) "His law is moral, not physical, a government of motive and not of force. It is vain to talk of his omnipotence preventing sin; if infinite motives cannot prevent it, it cannot be prevented, under a moral government, and to maintain the contrary, is to maintain a contradiction," (Finney's Sermons on important subjects, p. 58.)

Hence no faith can be exercised in the omnipotence of God by his praying people; in a moral universe, omnipotence has no potency; it cannot prevent sin; it cannot renew the wills of men. Omnipotence has been resisted by men and angels, and can be again. If men are unwilling to be saved, Omnipotence cannot make them willing. Omnipotence is altogether out of the question, in saving men; if God cannot gain the consent of men to be saved, by strong arguments, the effort must prove abortive; he cannot save them at all; he cannot "make them willing in the day of his power," but only in the day of their power, and when they are pleased to exercise it aright.

Saints may not persevere, they are not "kept by by the power of God, through faith, unto salvation," but by motives, and motives are, in their own nature resistable, have been resisted, and may be resisted again; and the saint may resist them, and perish.

Elect angles, and the spirits of just men made perfect, are moral agents held in obedience, not in the least degree, by omnipotence, but by motives alone, and they too can rebel, and may at any time break away from every restraint, sunder every holy tie, falsify every solemn covenant, rob Christ of his reward, the Spirit of his glory, and heaven of its inhabitants. If Omnipotence cannot prevent sin, if the heavenly hosts can thwart the will and power of Almighty God, if they choose to do so, who can tell but that the period may come when they will all abuse this dangerous power, and silence at once the hallelulias of heaven, and turn their backs upon the blessed Lamb, and leave the magnificent courts of Jehovah's temple desolate and forsaken? Oh, how profoundly dark and repulsive is this cheerless theory, when it thus unsettles the deep foundations of the everlasting covenant, and commits the perpetuity and glory of the heavenly state to a mere contingency.

These errors are all concatinated; they all arise from one, or, perhaps, two naked assumptions, viz.: first, that all holiness consists in the love of being in general, or in disinterested benevolence; and, secondly, that obligation, is in all cases, limited by ability. The former commences all moral distinctions, with the commencement of moral preferences, and turns mere nature into mere capability. The latter excludes the work of the spirit, and makes man independent of his maker in the work of obedience.

They are by no means self-evident propositions; they rest on no support from the word of God, and the system, therefore, which arises legitimately out of them, is woven, warp, and woof, from the imaginations of men. Though relied upon as primary moral principles, too clear to need any proof, yet, they are a mere begging of the question, mere assumptions, which never have been proved, and which never can be. Nay, their very results, prove them false, and stamp them with infamy, and give them up to reproach, show them to be, not the first principles of eternal truth, but the first principles in a connected tissue of error and false philosophy. These grapes never grew on Mount Zion, they are grapes of gall, their clusters are bitter.

In their incipiency, these propositions, and the speculations concerning them, produced but little alarm, and few comprehended their tendencies. Good men held them as axioms, but left them to their repose, as containing matters too metaphysical for the common mind, and continued to preach the gospel: but since they have become matured into system, the vampire is at the seat life, it fastens itself on the jugular vein in the neck of the church, and drains the vital current from all its members : it must be destroyed or it will destroy the church. Error has affinities for nothing but itself, and whenever it attains to entire self-consistency, in all its parts, it will have rejected every evangelical truth. The rapid growth of universalism, deism, and skepticism, around us, is traceable directly to this source, men have learned to depend upon reason, not upon revelation. Religious teachers have appealed almost exclusively to *common sense to first principles* and to the *nature of things* in proof of their positions. Their hearers have learned also to do the same, and the word of God has been brought into great contempt ; so that to prove a doctrine by the Bible, is become of no avail with many professing Christians ; if it cannot be proved by reason it cannot be proved at all.

Exposition has, to an alarming extent, also been supplanted by moral essays and philosophical speculations. "The people see not their signs ;" The house of prayer is sadly neglected, and the halls of false teachers thronged by the children of the church. Few seem to comprehend the cause of the deep and dreadful declension. But when imputation, atonement, depravity, and regeneration—these great pillars of christianity, exist only in name, or expire upon the rack of metaphysical inquisitors, or, at the least, are withheld from having utterance in the house of God, then there is a cause, a great and sufficient cause. The shield is upon the face of the sun, and it darkens the whole world. And when the gospel testimony is silent, or exhausted of its meaning, in the very church itself, is not this the time for error to set in from other quarters also, and to pour out its dark tides from the mouth of the dragon, and from the mouth of the beast, and from the mouth of the false prophet, and to bear away everything "lovely and of good report?"

Is this the time, then, for the cry of peace, and for the feeling of security? Is this the time? when error is already matured into system, and occupies the high places of Zion, and Deists, and Unitarians, are hailing its champions over the broken walls of the city of God. Nay, if it were some "time hallowed absurdity" which was made the object of assault, we might well be silent, but it is the faith once delivered to the saints. Not that faith as it exists in forms of government, and in forms of worship, but as it exists in its inmost sanctuary, arrayed in its sacerdotal robes, and sheding forth its spirit's blessed ministrations. And is this the time, then, for the witnesses to be silent and to suffer obscurity, to break their courage, and reproach to break their hearts? No, verily, there are principles involved in this controversy too sacred to be abandoned without a struggle, and which will never be abandoned by the friends of Zion. "If I forget thee, oh Jerusalem, let my right hand forget, if I do not prefer thee above my chief joy."

The errors which now assail the old-fashioned theology and impress upon the minds of the rising generation, a refined and philosophic infidelity, have been insidiously introduced and spread. They come from the most unexpected sources and take us by surprise; we cannot believe our eyes, or ears, nor listen to our uncharitable suspicions, we fear we may be doing injustice to men much better than ourselves, and await the result, till the most favorable period for successful resistance is already past, and the Son of Man is betrayed into the hands of sinners. The professions are sound, but the teachings are false and deceptive; creeds, sacred to the memory of reformers and martyrs, are in current use, but the philosophy of christianity, it is contended, is the wide open common which lies between truth and error, the neutral territory between Christ and Belial; this is the place for the tournaments, and here it is where helmets are broken, and the sword of the spirit vilely cast away. Nothing must be said, lest we should disturb the peace of Zion and arrest the progress of revivals. Alarm is uncalled for as no evil is intended; and none can accrue to the church from these innocent speculations; until, at length, the speculations have been turned into doctrines, and "truth has fallen in the streets and equity cannot enter."

For the last ten years, it is claimed, that correct views have revived and made great progress among the New School, and that, because the new measures have nearly disappeared from among them. But the new measures are but a small portion of the evils of which we complain, the doctrinal errors with which they were connected, and which they served to spread, were the germ of the apostacy, and they alone rendered them formidable. Error is usually cold and philosophical and cannot long continue to feed any excitement, good or bad; its first outporings are the melted lava which soon ceases to flow and lingers into rock; the religion which has succeeded to the new measures is, to a sad extent, a religion without revivals, and without the gospel. It is the new divinity, therefore, thus rapidly and silently diffusing itself everywhere, which awakens alarm and calls for kind but determined expostulation. The slumbers of the church must be broken, and that at any hazard. No mere managing of a few sound men, to outmanage their more wily foes, will avail aught in this struggle. "The children of this world are wiser in their generations, than the children of light." No cunningly devised method of preaching orthodoxy in terms so soft, and sweet, and ambiguous, as not to offend Pelagian hearers, will suit at all the exigencies of 'this evil day. The gospel must be preached as it was, and as it is; we are not sent to bury its lustre under velvet cushions, or to turn its edge with the down of thistles; we may keep our places by our pliancy, but we shall betray our trust and offend the master. "For do I now persuade men, or God; or do I seek to please men?" for if I yet pleased men, I should not be the servant of Christ." (Gal. 1—10.)

Reader, has curiosity led you to keep me company thus far, and are you yet in the broad and thronged way which leads to death? Think not then that error in the church diminishes in aught the guilt of your own unbelief, or delays for a moment your approaching doom. Justice, eternal justice demands your blood, and no arm can save you, but his who hung upon the tree. Your inability to obey the law is not your excuse, but the evidence of your guilt and deep necessity, and the harbinger of approaching ruin. Offended justice has no reluctant heart and no reluctant hand to punish.— "God shall wound the head of his enemies, and the hairy scalp of such an one as goeth on still in his tresspass." (Ps. xviii. 21;) darker still, and darker is the hue of guilt, deeper still, and deeper is the frown of injured heaven at the continued slight, put by your continued impenitence upon the only redeemer of God's elect. "Oh, if the word spoken by angels was steadfast and every transgression and disobedience received a just recompence of reward; How shall we escape if we neglect so great salvation." Heb. ii. 2, 3.

We call upon you therefore, by the truth of your total depravity, and by your righteous and hopeless condemnation in your present state; by the blood of atonement so long neglected, and by the expostulations of the Spirit so long resisted; in view of the resurrection morn, the judgement seat of Christ and the retributions of eternity, to awaken at once to righteousness and to cast yourself to day upon the bosom of your blessed and only Redeemer. The law condemns; justice demands your blood; conscience accuses, and your adversary the devil, seeks to devour. But Christ is the trembling sinners friend—kind to her taken in the very act of sin, and accused by all—near to him, who stands afar off, and smites upon his breast ; *he* upbraideth not—no bitter reproaches salute the ear of the prodigal ; his return lends speed to aged limbs, and grey locks stream upon the wind to meet him, while yet afar off—the words of self reproach are stifled by embraces, and the tears of bitterness are kissed away ; as it is written, " before they call I will answer, and while they are yet speaking I will hear." Isa. lxv. 24.— " Now then we are ambassadors for Christ as though God did beseech you by us, we pray you in Christ's stead, be ye reconciled to God for he hath made him to be sin for us, who knew no sin, that we might be made the righteousness of God in him." 2 Cor. v. 20. 21.

CHAPTER IX.

BASIS OF UNION AMONG PRESBYTERIANS.

What it is—The New School have departed from it—A return necessary to a union.

The Holy Spirit is represented as building a spiritual temple upon the foundation of the Apostles and prophets in which Jesus Christ occupies the place of the chief corner stone.— Eph. ii. 20. The foundation is doctrinal, and the distinguishing doctrine is that of the atonement of Christ, on this the whole superstructure ultimately rests. Every one also who reaches his destined place on this foundation, reaches it by an agency external to himself. The marble blocks repose in total insensibility in their native beds, here they are found by the architect, broken from the quarry, polished after the similitude of a palace, and borne to their place in the edifice. It occurs not to them to throw off their natural deformity and to go forth in beauty and usefulness. " They *are* builded," are wholly passive in taking their shape and in reaching their places.

The building is gradually completed. "Forty and six years was this temple in building," said the Jews of theirs. That of Diana, say some, was four hundred years in building ; but that of Jehovah has been in progress six thousand years, and ages yet to come, will roll away before the last elected stone shall be broken from natures quarry, and fitted and carried up "with shoutings of grace, grace unto it." Zech. iv. 9.

The doctrines of the gospel are as essential to a church state, as foundations are to a building. "If the foundations are destroyed what can the righteous do." The invisible church comprises in it the whole family of believers in heaven, and on earth of every nation and of every name; the visible church comprises in it, the various organizations of professed Christians who receive the doctrines of the gospel in a sufficient degree to enjoy a church state. A building may be supported by an imperfect foundation: the chief corner stone may be there, and many more of great utility, while the places of others may be supplied by wood, hay, stubble, and other worthless and combustable materials and yet the building may stand; its safety and durability is indeed greatly endangered, but its existence is not destroyed.

Some portions of the family of Christ are more visibly and sufficiently on this foundation, than others; and while a general fellowship should exist among these, yet none should be required to abandon their conscientious views of truth for the sake of union. A union effected in this manner would be unscriptural and injudicious. It is expected of Christians that they be honest men, and that they hold connection with that denomination whose peculiarities resemble most in their judgment the apostolic model. Their position in the visible church should be expressive of their conscientious convictions, and it can be no violation of the principles of an enlightened charity in them to require all who unite with them to embrace their denominational peculiarities.

As a portion of the church of Christ, we have expressed our views of the gospel in a compendious way. They are contained in our confession of faith and form of government, and in the larger and shorter catechisms of the Westminster Assembly of divines; while we do not maintain that we are the church of Christ exclusive of all others, we still insist on an honest subscription to our standards, on the part of all those who unite with us, and we believe our course, in this respect, to be in accordance with common usage, with enlightened charity, and essential to our existence as a Christian church.

A union of all denominations in one body, while each one should be permitted to maintain its peculiar views, would awaken bitter controversy, and result in mutual alienation. Socialism has not yet proved that one house is large enough for more than one family, and the enlightened lovers of harmony in the churches will not attempt to prove it.

A union, also, in which a silent abandonment of mutual differences in opinion should be agreed upon, would involve in it a criminal dereliction of principle, and a total abandonment of the gospel. Churches are bound to a solemn and earnest testimony to what they believe to be the truth, and they cannot be released by any conventional arrangements whatever. The differences which separate believers into denominations, are various, and, though each communion may receive a sufficient amount of evangelical truth to preserve the integrity of their church state, yet, when each one shall have relinquished all their differences with every other, the denomination which would be the result would have but little to distinguish it from an association of free thinkers. Take, for example, those differences which separate Old from New School Presbyterians, alone, for an illustration of this point. One believes that Christ endured the penalty of the law; another, that he did not. One that he obeyed it for his people; the other that he obeyed it for himself. One that his righteousness is imputed to believers; the other that it is not, but that the act of faith is imputed. One that faith receives the righteousness of Christ; the other that Christ needs it for himself. One that regeneration is an act of God; the other that it is the act of man. One that it is a change of nature; the other that it is a change of purpose. One that man can do nothing, of himself; the other that he can do everything, which is required, of himself. And thus we might proceed to include other denominations, and to show, that if we should agree to relinquish our respective differences for the sake of a common union with each other, we should, in that event, agree to relinquish every evangelical truth, everything held dear and sacred by any. We might retain the names of christian doctrines, but no explanation could be attempted of their meaning without breaking the principles of the compact. The points on which we differ are so numerous, extending so, to every doctrine of the gospel, and so, to every explanation of every doctrine; no one thing would more effectually destroy our entire Christianity than an amalgamation, on such conditions; every minister would become silent, every pulpit vacant; every church empty. Such an union ought never to be proposed, or if proposed, ought, promptly and unanimously, to be rejected.

As Presbyterians, therefore, we have but one course left for us to pursue—but one basis of union to present. Our infallible rule of faith and practice, is the Bible, our epitome of it, is the confession of faith. In that instrument our views of christianity are fully stated, without reserve, and without ambiguity; and if the New School desire a union with us, they ought first to retract their errors, and to make an honest subscription to our standards. We ought to exact no less from them; they ought to expect no less from us. A condemnation of the act of 1837, on our part, would not restore the breach, for the plain and sufficient reason, that it did not make it. To approve or condemn it, is not, with us, an article of faith, or a condition of union. We do not believe in the infallibility of Ecumenical Councils, or of General Assemblies; we believe that the plan of union, because never consented to by the several Presbyteries, was unwise, and unconstitutional, and that from its injurious operation, its abrogation was imperiously demanded, by every principle of self preservation. But whether our views on this subject, are correct or not, can be of but small moment, since, whether the act of '37 was wise or unwise, it could not dissolve our organization, or separate any one from the Presbyterian church; each one has but to comply with the order and direction of the Assembly, and avail himself of the provisions made for him in the act itself, by uniting with the nearest contiguous presbytery, and every difficulty is overcome. The declaration of war with Mexico, may have been an error of the administration, but the effect of it was not a dissolution of the Federal Compact. On the war question, our citizens will hold different opinions, and will remain good citizens still; and with respect to the plan of union and its abrogation we may entertain very different opinions, and be good Presbyterians still. Our particular opinions concerning the *acts* of the general assembly, have as little to do with the basis of union among Presbyterians, as the Mexican war has to do with the general confederacy. We are not to expect perfection in any administration, but we ought to expect loyalty on the part of every subject. Secession is rebellion. An honest subscription to our standards, is therefore, most reasonably required, and most certainly expected. To talk or think of any other method of union, is idle. The door is already thrown open, as wide as it ought, and as wide as it can be.

The New School have seceded from the church, denied to her, her distinctive missionary character, and changed her form of government. But above all their leading men, Dr's. Cox, Beman, Beecher, Duffield, and Mr. Barnes, have denied the great doctrines of the gospel as understood and explained by Presbyterians, and these denials have taken a permanent, popular form, and have obtained a wide circulation; communicants and their children are alienated from the church of their fathers, and have learned to speak lightly of the faith of the martyrs, and of the witnesses of Jesus. Imputation, original sin, native depravity, regeneration and atonement, are beginning to have existence only in name; all that these great doctrines imply, is treated by many, as the idle philosophy of the Schools. In these serious and fundamental questions, they have departed from us; and if they desire a union, let them first restore the breach they have made. The evidences that they are the offenders against union, and that they renew the offence, and keep up the feud, meet us every where. Their protection of errorists, and the wide circulation which they are still giving to their dangerous opinions, prove that, whatever else they may be, they are not Presbyterians. Their unwillingness to separate from the General Assembly, by compromise—their abrupt breaking off of kind negociations, and their suit at law, which originated wholly with themselves, prove their spirit to have been any other than brotherly or peaceable, at the time. The decision of the court, that they were not the General Assembly of the Presbyterian Church, in the United States, and their failure to prosecute their appeal to a higher court, prove that the laws of our country, and their own ominous failures, are against the justice of their claims;—intimates that their cause is wanting in integrity, is wholly indefensible on its own merits, and, on this account, needs to be supported by the war of prejudices, raised upon false issues. So that in every aspect of the whole question, they are evidently the aggressors; and if they sincerely desire, or expect a union with us, they should at once return to the point at which they commenced their separation. They have departed, let them return. They have made the breach, let them restore it. They have entered the bosom of our peaceful family, and bred heresy, strife and debate, in it. They have entered our well-tilled garden, and trodden in the dust the rose of sharon, and the lily of the valley there. They have broken down our hedges, led away our children, and decoyed our people. They have done the evil, therefore, to make reparation, belongs to them. The basis of union remains as aforetime: The confession of faith, and the form of government, and the longer and shorter chatechisms of the Westminster Assembly of Divines, are not altered.

But if the New School have improved upon the old basis and taken away some of its bad principles, and supplied their place with better ones, then it behooves us to follow them as they more perfectly follow Christ. In this conslusion we concur. But is it an improvement to destroy the appellate jurisdiction, and missionary character of the General Assembly? To deny that Christ obeyed the law and bore its curse for his people? To maintain that the act of faith, and not the righteousness of Christ, is imputed to us, for our justification? That God's immutable law is changed? that he does not require of fallen man, what he did require of him in his state of primeval innocence? That men are able to keep the law, to repent and believe the gospel, without the aid of the Holy Ghost? That human nature is not depraved? That infants are not the subjects of moral government? And that God does nothing for man in regeneration, that he cannot do for himself? These are alterations of our creed, but are they improvements simply on that account? That is to assume the very thing to be proved, or to assume that the gospel is, in its own nature, a progressive development of truth, and that change is prima facie evidence of desirable amendment and progress.

The works of creation are finished works, they remain just what they were six thousand years ago, the face of the heavens, the sun, the moon, the stars, the revolutions of the earth, the changes of the seasons, the atmosphere, the clouds, the wind, the dew, the rain, all remain just what they were when they were first made. They are incapable of change for the better, as they are already beautifully adapted to their end—the perfected works of God, and any alteration of their constitution would endanger the safety of the world. The gospel, also, in like manner, is a finished testimony. The heavens that now overhang the new Jerusalem, are just what they were eighteen hundred years ago. They have not changed, and they never will while time shall last. The balmy atmosphere which at first surrounded Mount Zion, surrounds it still, unchanged. The dew that glitters like a shower of diamonds there, falls and shines and refreshes as aforetime. And the sun of righteousness still looks down from the same spot in the firmament, and bathes the city of the great king in the same softened effulgence as at the first. All things here retain their primeval sweetness and glory, unimpaired and unimproved. The doctrines of the gospel are as incapable of change for the better as are the works of nature; and any alteration of them endangers the welfare of the souls of men.

But, if it be said, that although the gospel cannot be improved, yet that this is not true of the confession of faith,—I reply, then, that this may be true, and, as the New School profess to have made great improvements, why have they not incorporated them in their new confession of faith? I find some changes in church government in that instrument, but they are themselves already out of patience with these very changes. These, then, cannot be intended, and as they have made no formal changes in our doctrinal standards, wherein have they made any improvement at all? They profess to believe the confession of faith; that it is strictly in accordance with the word of God; that it requires no change, and that their improvements are in the mere philosophy of Christianity; that these are wholly unimportant in their nature, and should not alienate us from each other. Why, then, in the name of charity, do they make such a great ado about so great a trifle, and finally rend the church from Maine to Texas for a mere figment, the mere moonshine of philosophy? "Why did the best beloved Brutus stab if not for justice?" If it be not for Christianity itself, then abandon it at once. If this mere philosophy, be a mere nothing, it will cost them nothing to forsake it; to remove in the true spirit of christian conciliation, and condecension, this abomination that maketh desolate, and to restore union, and harmony, and confidence among alienated brethren. Thus the very defences set up by the New School, are the evidences of conscious weakness, and resemble the excuses and subterfuges of a defeated party, and of a failing cause.

A church is a company of living witnesses to the truth, and her creed is one of the forms in which she embodies and exhibits her testimony. If she simply declared her belief in the scriptures, and did not state definitely, what she understood the scriptures to teach, her testimony could not be distinguished from that of errorists; for all Protestant denominations of every grade, believe that the word of God, contained in the scriptures of the old and new testaments, is the only infallible rule of faith and practice. The line of demarcation, between a true and a false Christianity, commences with formal statements of our faith— with distinct, and clear definitions of our views. Here, at this point, it is that the church emerges from the confusion of tongues, and makes her sound and sanctifying testimony. To profess that she believes the scriptures, and to do no more, would not be a mark of fidelity, would not make her either conspicuous or useful,—"a city set on a hill which cannot be hid." She must declare what the scriptures teach, as to "what we are to believe concerning God, and what duty God requires of man." Her creed, her catechism, her living ministry, must keep back nothing deemed "profitable for doctrine, for reproof, for correction, and for instruction in righteousness."

In this duty the Presbyterian Church has been remarkable for her firmness and fidelity. She has a creed, and one very difficult either to prevert or misunderstand. It is not rejected because its true meaning, lies deeply hid among metaphysical mists and antiquated theological technicalities; because friged as the poles and "dark as Erebus and old night" and its meaning impossible to be comprehended. It is rejected because it is understood too well—because it is warm with holy fire, and filled with unearthly majesty and uncompromising truth. It is hated and rejected for the same reasons that the gospel, of which it is a beautiful epitome, is hated and rejeced,—because it embodies and presents that gospel in its well defended and admirable proportions.

Our testimony is one, with that of the apostles, and one, with that of their successors. We teach the same gospel which Paul taught to the Roman's, to the Galatians, to the Hebrews,—we unite with the church in the wilderness in reiterating her testimony, and with the subsequent army of reformers and martyrs and witnesses of Jesus, in theirs. We do not regard Christianity as a progressive science, but as a perfected revelation; we promulgate no new doctrines; we usurp no authority over the conciences of men; we maintain the ancient gospel and the headship of Christ over his own house.

The church in all ages is the same, and her testimony is the same. That testimony has been as well understood, as clearly stated, as deeply loved, as highly valued, as ably defended by the witnesses of Jesus in other days, as it now is. We have gained nothing by time and distance, by progress in commerce, in arts, and arms over them. They gazed upon the same heavens that we gaze upon, inhaled the same atmosphere, were informed by the same spirit, and were built upon the same foundations: "seeing then that we are compassed about by so great a crowd of witnesses, let us lay aside every weight and the sin that doth so easily beset us, and let us run with patience the race set before us, looking unto Jesus the author and finisher of our faith." Brethren other foundation can no man lay than that is laid, which is Jesus Christ, in his penal sufferings, imputed righteousness and spirits ministration: and to be rooted and grounded in the truth, as it is in Him, is no ordinary blessing. But to be separated from it—to be ever learning and never able to come to the knowledge of the truth, is an affliction grievous to bear, a sad ingredient in the cup of bitterness. To break from our moorings here, is to wander about at all uncertainties, the sport of every unquiet wave and contrary wind; back to this point we shall look with a tearful eye and with an aching heart, remembering the days of an uncorrupted simplicity, and of a settled faith. Then a false philosophy had not as yet spread out her dark pall upon the bosom of our perished hopes, nor filled the sunny sky with a perpetual gloom ; but since we have listened to that wily foe, who hath cast down many strong men, wounded, our eyes are darkened, and we cannot say that we have a lie in our right hand.

But if we have wandered, there is a pathway of return. Those however, who reach the foundation *are* built upon it. No native strength or righteousness can build us on that foundation. Without the Spirit's aid we can neither find it, nor reach it, if it were found. The Holy Spirit breaks the rock from the quarry, and fits and polishes and bears it to its place on the foundation, none shall make any progress toward that place of security and repose, without a sufficient knowledge of this blessed truth. The more fully we understand and appreciate our inability and our entire dependence on the Holy Ghost, the brighter is the hope of a successful return. "Work out, therefore, your own salvation, with fear and trembling, for it is God that worketh in you both to will and to do of his good pleasure." Amen.

CHAPTER X.

PLEA FOR UNION AMONG PRESBYTERIANS.

A union desirable—Division among Christians an evil—The true remedy proposed.

Our Lord prays for a union among his followers in all ages, "neither pray I for these alone, but for them also, which shall believe on me through their word, that they all may be one, as thou Father art in me and I in thee, that they also may be one in us, that the world may believe that thou hast sent me." The union is desirable. The prayer for it was offered up by our Lord, just before he was betrayed. It is his dying request; and this fact presents the subject to us, with additional solemnity, and impressiveness. The union for which he prayed included at least the following particulars.

A union in nature.—That the church might possess in common, "the divine nature," (2 Pet. i. 4.) The holiness of God, not in degree, but in kind, being "renewed in righteousness and true holiness, after the image of Him who created man.

A spiritual union.—The same spirit renewing, sanctifying, and dwelling in them all, making the whole church one, by distributing to each one the inhabitation of the same Holy Spirit.

A union in the affections of the heart, and in the views of the mind; they "being perfectly joined together in the same mind, and in the same judgment."

It was desired that this union should be visible, and tend

to the conversion of the world: "that the world may believe that thou hast sent me."

There are popular virtues, which, when seen in the church, secure the confidence and respect of mankind, and have a bearing on their conversion. "Let your light so shine before men, that they, seeing your good works, may glorify your Father who is in heaven." Union among believers is one of these, because so opposite to the spirit of the world, and so delightful an exhibition of the harmony of heaven. Behold, how good, and how pleasant it is, to see brethren dwell together in unity: it is like the dew, that descended upon the mountains of Zion : for there the Lord commanded the blessing, even life for evermore. Psalm cxxxiii.

Wars and fightings are in the world; men are hateful, and hate one another; each one would be greatest. An equal, a superior, a rival, cannot be endured. Men are "desirous of vain glory, provoking one another, envying one another;" but when we meet with those who are united in a church state, and have fervent charity among themselves—united in one heart and one mind—the contrast is striking, and we meet it with an agreeable surprise. We turn often to it, as weary mortals turn from the heartless glitter of wealth and fashion, from the pride of cultivated intellect, from the rage for gold and preferment, to the period of youthful innocence, the sweet recollection of happier days, and desire to dwell in a spot so hallowed, in which Heaven has blotted out the animosities of the past, and opened upon the ravished sight, the delightful visions of the future.

Union among Christians, in their testimony, gives that testimony greater credibility and force. The Church is a company of witnesses to the truth, and it is desirable that that testimony should, in no respect, be conflicting or contradictory. "We are his witnesses of these things, and so is also the Holy Ghost, whom God hath given to all them that obey him." This testimony began, at the first, to be spoken by

the Son, and was confirmed unto us, by them that heard him.
They confirmed the testimony of Christ, by repeating it
without contradiction or alteration, and to verify the truth
of their testimony, another witness also appeared, "God also
bearing them witness, both with signs and wonders, and divers miracles, and gifts of the Holy Ghost, according to his
will." Paul multiplies the witnesses to the same Gospel, that
he may increase the force of his own testimony. In the xi.
chapter of his epistle to the Hebrews, he unites himself with
all the intermediate witnesses to the Gospel, back to the time
of Abel. He calls out the stars, one by one, till at length
they are gathered, and mingle in a vast galaxy, and surround
the city of the living God, with a subduing and refreshing
brightness. Thus he places the city on a hill; it shines from
afar, over whole countries, and along the flight of ages; the
mellow light in which it reposes, attracts us away from the
evanescent glare of all earthly glory, to gaze upon its surpassing and attractive loveliness; "beautiful for situation,
yea, the joy of the whole earth, is Mount Zion, on the sides
of the north, the city of the great King, God is known for a
refuge in her palaces."

The divisions of the Church of Christ, therefore, into separate organizations, each delivering its separate and conflicting testimony, tends greatly to weaken the force of that testimony, and to obscure its lustre. Her testimony is stronger
or weaker in proportion as she is more or less united in it.—
Her want of union is an evil to be deplored, and in every aspect in which it can be viewed, it is an evil. God brings
light out of darkness, and good out of evil—He overruled
the wickedness of Joseph's brethren to good, and the murder
of his Son, to the salvation of men; and he overrules the
divisions in the Church, to a more full examination, and a
more perfect understanding of his word, and to various other
desirable ends. But these acts of his providence do not interfere with the nature of evil actions: they remain evil still;

no good results growing out of divisions in churches, can prove that they are in themselves innocent, or that they ought to be desired on their own account.

These divisions are not modern; they originated with a primitive Christianity, and will continue till the fullness of the Gentiles be come in; then shall the Jews return, and there shall be but one fold and one Shepherd. Our Lord did not regard division as innocent, but as inevitable, in the present state of knowledge and holiness: "it must needs be that offences come, but woe unto him by whom the offence cometh." Judaizing teachers formed large parties and corrupted and divided the primitive churches. . Their conduct met with severe reprehension from the Apostle Paul—"Mark them which make divisions and offences, contrary to the doctrine ye have learned, and avoid them, for they that be such serve not our Lord Jesus Christ, but their own lusts, and by good words and fair speeches deceive the hearts of the simple." At Ephesus, he called for the elders of the church, and said. "after my departure, shall grievous wolves enter in among you, not sparing the flock, and of your own selves shall men arise, speaking perverse things, and leading away disciples after them." The spirit of Antichrist had also begun to operate, even in his day, "whose coming was after the working of Satan, with all power, and signs, and lying wonders, and with all deceivableness of unrighteousness in them that perish."

But the power which preserved the bush unconsumed, amid the flame, preserves the church likewise, amid the rage of conflicting opinions. The arm which sustained the bride in the wilderness, sustains her still. "The sea has come up upon Babylon"—Tyre. Sidon and Ninevah, have disappeared with her beneath the angry wave; there the crescent is sinking fast, and there, in the eddies of the same maelstrom, appears the mother of abominations, hurrying with increasing violence, toward the devouring gorge. But the church, though frail as a helpless woman, abandoned in her light shallop, on the crest of the thundering surge, shall ride securely amid the war of elements, and play with the main of the sea, and out-live the fearful storm, in which steamers are wrecked, and navies dismasted. Christ is with her, and however great her perils, she can never be engulfed and lost.

Two remedies have been alternately tried to cure the evils of disunion. The one has dispensed with persuasion, and insisted on uniformity by pains and penalties. The other has made its seductive appeal to the law of a false charity. The former has procured a union as heartless and false, as the means resorted to were cruel and unscriptural. The latter has made a fair show in the flesh, but has tended to apostacy. It has required us to abandon our differencs, and to love one another, to care less about doctrine, and more about union— in other words, to care less about christianity, and more about harmony; for christianity is not christianity, without its doctrines. No reformation, however, which has been finally acknowledged to have been from heaven, has ever taken this direction. The Holy Spirit never leads us to be indifferent to the truth, in order that we may return to God, and imbibe more of the love and harmony of heaven.

The great revival of religion among the Israelites, when they came out of Egypt, was a revival of knowledge, and gracious affections. They had fallen into great ignorance, and irreligion, in Egypt, and for a whole year divine knowledge was shed upon them from the burning mount. The reformation went in the direction of truth, and toward God. A revival of indifference to truth, in the churches, is the work of satan, and the harmony, which is the result of it, is that which pervades the palace of "the strong man armed;" he is the ruler of the darkness of this world, or of its spiritual ignorance; it is his appropriate domain; here he erects his gloomy throne, and sways his infernal scepter, and reigns; for if our gospel be hid, it is hid to them that are lost, in whom the God of this world hath blinded the minds of them that believe not, lest the light of the knowledge of the glory of Christ, who is the image of God, should shine unto them."

The great revival which commenced the Christian era, was a war upon error, accompanied by the propagation of truth in spirit and in power. Judaism, and Paganism, and every form of false philosophy, and of false religion, met in Christianity a determined antagonist. It sent not peace on earth, but a sword—it broke the harmony of hell, to introduce the harmony of heaven. The revival was a revival of truth and purity, not of union, produced by a compromise with errorists, and by indifference to the word of God. Christ came to break in upon the kingdom, supported and swayed by erroneous opinions, and to turn mankind from darkness to light, and from the power of Satan unto God.

The revival of the sixteenth century, was not a compromise between conflicting sectaries, but a revival of the great doctrines of Christianity, long buried beneath the errors of Pelagius, and the consequent superstitions of Rome. The reformers recovered and reopened the word of God, and revived the long neglected testimony of Jesus. The result was glorious and the gracious work abiding.

Whenever any great religious movement is from heaven, it will inevitably be attended with an increasing attachment to the gospel, to its peculiar spirit, and to its peculiar truths ; for by this instrumentality hath it pleased God "to save them that believe." In a genuine revival of religion, men "will not be ashamed of the gospel of Christ, nor be disposed to undervalue any of its doctrines, "for it is the power of God unto salvation, unto every one that believeth." To unite by compromise, would be to give up all that would make a union valuable—indeed, it would be to relinquish the very union itself, for the sake of a union, to agree to remain in perpetual disunion, by agreeing never to discuss our differences. No such union exists between the Father, and Son, and Holy Spirit; nor did our Lord pray for such a union among his disciples ; neither can it be shown that he commands, or approves it. "Come out from among them and be ye separate, saith the Lord God, and touch not the unclean thing, for what communion hath light with darkness, or what concord hath Christ with Belial, or he that believeth with an infidel. The remedy proposed, is indeed, worse than the disease it is intended to cure. It will be far better that we should remain as we are, than that we should abandon the gospel for the sake of a union which would exist only in appearance and not in heart. If we should correct our errors, and become of one heart, and one mind, then a union would be real, and of a most happy tendency. That such a union should be created and maintained, was the desire of our blessed Lord, when he said, " That they all may be one as thou Father art in me, and I in thee, that they may be one in us, that the world may believe that thou hast sent me."

The grand remedy, then, for division, is to elevate among ourselves the standard of orthodoxy and piety. True Christianity is not many, but one, in her nature, spirit, and affinities. Let each division of the church, therefore, approximate this common standard, more and more ; and in this manner will all their mutual differences vanish gradually, and ultimately disappear altogether. "Those things which are equal to the same thing, are equal to one another." This is an axiom, whose truth would be beautifully illustrated, by the perfect conformity of all denominations to the scripture model, then like kindred drops they would be one—equal to the same thing, they would be equal to one another. The union of Christians, therefore, into one body, will be sure to prove impracticable, and unprofitable, in the present condition of the churches. This blessed period must be postponed till our mutual differences vanish, by our more perfect approach and conformity to the common standard, then, when all shall see eye to eye, and lift up a united testimony, the church will wield the sword of the spirit, with greater energy and success, against the rulers of the darkness of this world, than in any former period of her history.

All denominational boundaries ought to be regarded as sacred; every minister, and every communicant ought to express, truthfully, their respective views, by their position in the visible church. It is not, alone, a question of usefulness, or policy, but also of common honesty, which is to be attended to in the profession of our faith. No man can, without a change in his sentiments, be an Old School Presbyterian, in one end of the state, and a New School Presbyterian in the other, and be an honest man. How can he if so flexible, expect to be either trusted, or respected among his brethren? He will be regarded as in the market to be bought for a piece of bread. It is to be hoped, that these pliable consciences will diminish in number; they are spots in our feasts of charity.

Those Old School men, who come into places where the New School have the majority, in wealth and influence, and unite with them on that account, must expect to lose cast with their former brethren; if they claim that they have changed their friends only, and not their sentiments, they publish their own shame. If they cannot endure affliction with their suffering brethren—if Presbyterians are not the same to them, whether in linsey woolsey, or in broad-cloth; whether in rags or robes, they are not to be trusted any where, can be no great acquisition to any party; and it is a blessing to any denomination, to be quit of all such unstable, not to say, unprincipled adherents.

Each denomination has a fixed character—that character belongs to all its members. We cannot give character to the denomination to which we belong, it must give character to us; if we unite with the New School body, or remain in it, and expect to be regarded as Old School men, our expectation is no compliment, either to our understanding, or to our integrity; our motives will be duly appreciated in the end, and our moral worth weighed in the balances. This view of the conduct of such triflers, is not peculiar to us; it is common to all denominations, and to the New School among the rest. We can respect the man whose position expresses his true convictions—whose "eye when turned on empty space, beams keen with honor"—who is an an epistle known and read of all men, even though we may esteem him to be in error; but "if he is not faithful in the unrighteous mammon, who will commit to him the true riches?" who can respect or trust him?

The third party which claims to be of no party, but to stand aloof, both from the New and Old School divisions of the church, are not believed to be what their professions imply. They are regarded as imbittered partizans, and they have become too zealous for neutrality, to be thought neutral any longer. Their tendency has never been to the union of Presbyterians, but to a new division of the church. There is however, no demand for a new division; all can find a home now, either with New or Old School bodies already organized, and occupying the same fields. These brethren must be difficult indeed to please, if a new denomination must be created on purpose, to make the greatest enemies of all division, a home by themselves. Their great disinterestedness, their great love of peace, should not turn them into a faction, so violent in its animosities, as to lead to a new rent in the seamless garment of the Master. If there had been no call for former divisions among Presbyterians, then surely there can be no call for the organization of an independent Synod in Western New York. I say this to take away the apology, from those who profess to be Old School Presbyterians, and yet refuse to unite with us, because they expect to have a third organization. I do not say it, to prevent such an organization—it needs nothing to prevent it, for it will never exist.

The very idea itself has almost ceased to amuse the fancy of any sober man, in the shape of a rational probability.

Finally, the opinions of other denominations, can never be our standard of truth and righteousness. We are not required to conform to them, but to the word of God, and however wide it may make the breach between us, and those who differ from us, we are nevertheless to walk by the same rule, to mind the same things. Paul would never have benefitted the church, if he had modified the truth to please men, nor shall we, if the great doctrines of the gospel which we receive, are not distinctly stated and defended. If the lust of numbers, shall at length prevail over the love of truth, and a union should be agreed upon, to any great extent, between the Pelagian and the Calvinistic bodies, there are thousands who would sit down and weep when they remember Zion, and look upon that period as the darkest, which the American Presbyterian church ever witnessed. But this period will we trust never arrive, there are no tendencies that way, each division of the church is becoming more homogeneous, more alike among themselves, and more perfectly unlike each other. These tendencies, are silently, but constantly opperating, and the result is becoming more and more palpable. It is a relief to know, that we are not to be called upon to fight over again the battles already so honorably won, to know that we may now pursue our high vocation as a church, without further or serious molestation. May we all "follow the things that make for peace and the things which edify one another." "How can two walk together except they be agreed," our plea then for union is for one, not simply in form, hollow and heartless, but for such a union as that desired in the prayer of the Master, "that they all may be one, as thou, Father art in me and I in thee, that they may be one in us." Amen.

www.ingramcontent.com/pod-product-compliance
Lightning Source LLC
Chambersburg PA
CBHW070314230426
43663CB00011B/2123